The Yerushalmi

The Yerushalmi—
The Talmud of the
Land of Israel:

An Introduction

JACOB NEUSNER

Jason Aronson Inc.
Northvale, New Jersey
London

The Library of Classical Judaism is a series of three volumes by
Dr. Jacob Neusner.

The Mishnah: An Introduction
The Midrash: An Introduction
The Yerushalmi—The Talmud of the Land of Israel: An Introduction

This book was set in 10/12 Divinne
by Alpha Graphics, Pittsfield, New Hampshire,
and printed and bound by Haddon Craftsmen of Scranton, Pennsylvania.

Library of Congress Cataloging-in-Publication Data

Neusner, Jacob, 1932-
  The Yerushalmi—the Talmud of the land of Israel : an introduction
/ Jacob Neusner.
     p. cm.
  Includes bibliographical references and index.
  ·ISBN 0-87668-812-1
  1. Talmud Yerushalmi—Introductions. 2. Justice, Administration
of (Jewish law) 3. Talmud Yerushalmi—Theology. 4. Talmud
Yerushalmi—Historiography. I. Title.
  BM498.8.N49 1991
  296.1'2406—dc20   91-19713
                                                     CIP

Manufactured in the United States of America. Jason Aronson Inc. offers books and
cassettes. For information and catalog write to Jason Aronson Inc., 230 Livingston Street,
Northvale, New Jersey 07647.

For my colleague and friend
Kristin S. Shrader-Frechette—
a token of esteem and affection

Contents

Preface

The Talmud of the Land of Israel, also called the Yerushalmi, arranged as a mere commentary to the Mishnah, forms one of the great unappreciated monuments to the life and culture of the Jewish people in the Land of Israel in the formative age of Judaism. Indeed, its pages record the formation of Judaism as the faith has been known from the fourth century C.E. to the present day. So much is at stake in an account of its literary, cultural, and religious summation of Israel, the Jewish people, living in the Land of Israel.

Yet it is practically unknown, commonly not studied in yeshivot in which "the Talmud" means "the Talmud of Babylonia," and certainly not consulted outside of yeshivot at all. So the Yerushalmi is to be compared to the Essene writings discovered at the Dead Sea in 1947. Now imagine for a moment that a hillside cave in Galilee, carved open to the light for the first time in millennia, yielded a vast library of hitherto unknown writings of ancient Judaism. Jar after jar of documents on blackened leather came forth. Once deciphered and published—a labor of many years—these leather pages turned out to discuss a known document, but to say quite new things about it, to speak in an unfamiliar idiom about already established rules.

Consider in your mind's eye the sensation such a discovery—the sudden, unanticipated discovery of the Yerushalmi—would cause, the scholarly lives and energies that would flow to the new find and its explication. Converging interests in not merely philology and history, but also the study of religions and the analysis of the roots of Western culture would contrive to make the new Galilean library a centerpiece of scholarly discourse for many decades. To call the contents of that hillside cave a revolution, to compare them to the finds at Qumran, at the Dead

Sea, or at Nag Hammadi, or to any of the other great contemporary discoveries from ancient times, would hardly be deemed an exaggeration.

The Yerushalmi (also called the "Palestinian Talmud" or "Talmud of the Land of Israel") is such a library. Comprising thirty-nine tractates, it fills many hundreds of pages with barely intelligible writing. Famous for its incomprehensibility, the document has come before the scholarly public in bits and pieces, odd pages snatched from an otherwise inaccessible Geniza. A paragraph here, a sentence there—these have been made to serve as representations of this odd and difficult work. The result is that the Yerushalmi as a whole, with its remarkably coherent and systematic statement, has yet to win sustained attention. Its testimony to the worldview and way of life of the people who made it up has gone unnoticed. The few Talmudists who took an interest sedulously protected their monopoly of knowledge, declaring all outsiders unclean for entry into the sanctum of learning.

Accordingly, with the completion of the first full translation of the Yerushalmi into a Western language (the French translation skips difficult passages), the Yerushalmi comes forth for the first time to the light of day to be viewed whole and complete by the generality of learned people. I refer to *The Talmud of the Land of Israel: A Preliminary Translation and Explanation* (Univ. of Chicago 1982-1989), I-XXXV, in thirty-five volumes, twenty-five translated by this writer, ten by others and edited by me. My twenty-five tractates are in print. While, as I said, a handful of Talmudists have long had access to bits and pieces, they mined underground, alone, in deep and barely accessible passages. They traded in a mysterious closed market whatever nuggets they retrieved. In any case, few spent much time in the depths of the Yerushalmi. With the breaking open of a strip mine, however imperfect for the moment, the whole vein for the first time is open to the light for all to see and plunder in the name of learning.

Known for sixteen hundred years, from the time of its closure and redaction, generally assumed to be the end of the fourth century and beginning of the fifth, C.E., the Yerushalmi has suffered an odious but deserved reputation for the difficulty in making sense of its discourse. That reputation is only partly true; there are many passages that are scarcely intelligible. But there are a great many more that are entirely or mainly accessible. And the document as a whole is now becoming available in a complete, if preliminary and occasionally uncertain, translation, on the basis of which I propose to accomplish the first historical-religious study of the document as a whole.

In this volume I deal with the character of the Yerushalmi as literature and then with the three most important doctrines that reach us now in the formulation that the authorship of the Yerushalmi imparted: the Judaic doctrines of the sages, Torah, and history. This is not to suggest that many other important components of Judaism have not come to us in the definition of the authorship of the Yerushalmi. But these are the most important, and, in introducing the Yerushalmi and what is important about it, I could think of no more fundamental and enduring conceptions than the ones I have identified.

It remains to explain the notation system that I have invented for the representation of the rabbinic literature. In ancient times punctuation as we know it was unknown. We supply punctuation to make the ancient texts accessible to ourselves. Throughout this book, Y. stands for Yerushalmi, and M. stands for Mishnah. Originally, there was no indication of sentences or paragraphs or chapter-headings. Until now, modern translations have presented chapters and paragraphs and sentences, but have not indicated, through a notation system, how we may conveniently refer to them. I mark what we should call a chapter with a roman numeral, which always corresponds to the enumeration system of the texts as printed in Hebrew. I then use an arabic numeral to mark a paragraph, and a letter to mark an individual sentence. In this way I not only make ready reference possible, I also indicate what I conceive to be the smallest whole units of thought, which we call sentences. These are sets of words that hold together to make a single coherent statement, that is, a statement of fact. Any further division within those sets of words will not yield a coherent statement at all, hence the lettered components of a composition. These groups of sentences ordinarily form coherent statements, which we should call paragraphs. The composites of lettered sentences then are marked with an arabic numeral, which indicates that, in my judgment, the components form a cogent whole. Then the groups of such composites form a still larger one, and that is, as I said, the one marked by a roman numeral. These notations therefore allow us to perceive immediately how a given composite is made up of its individual parts and how they relate to each other. No other translations of the rabbinic literature in any language provide notation system, which means that analysis of the translated document (all the more so the original Hebrew) is not possible. The advantages of my system are self-evident.

This book restates for the purpose of introducing the document studies of mine listed in the bibliography. I also refer there to the major bibliography of the Yerushalmi, which is Baruch M. Bokser's in *The Study of Ancient Judaism.* My thanks go to Arthur Kurzweil, of Jason Aronson Inc., for proposing this volume and helping me execute it, and to William Scott Green, of the University of Rochester, who discussed the work with me while I was doing it.

JACOB NEUSNER
University of South Florida
Tampa

Prologue

The Judaism of the Talmud of the Land of Israel forms one plank in the bridge that leads from antiquity to the beginning of the Middle Ages, from the Middle East to Europe, from the end of the classical age to the nascent moment of our own time and place. The Mishnah, in c. 200 C.E., describes an orderly world in which Israelite society is neatly divided among its castes, arranged in priority around the center that is the Temple, systematically engaged in a life of sanctification remote from the disorderly events of the day. The Yerushalmi, in c. 400 C.E., portrays the chaos of Jews living among Gentiles, governed by a diversity of authorities, lacking all order and arrangement, awaiting a time of salvation for which, through sanctification, they make themselves ready. The Mishnah's Israel in imagination is governed by an Israelite king, high priest, and Sanhedrin. The Yerushalmi's Jews lived under both rabbis near at hand, who settled the everyday disputes of the streets and households, and also under distant archons of a nameless state, to be manipulated and placated on earth as in heaven. The Mishnah's Judaism breathes the pure air of public piazza and stoa, the Yerushalmi's, the ripe stench of private alleyway and courtyard. The image of the Mishnah's Judaism is evoked by the majestic Parthenon, perfect in all its proportions, conceived in a single moment of pure rationality. The Yerushalmi's Judaism is an inchoate cathedral in process, the labor of many generations, each of its parts the conception of diverse moments of devotion, all of them the culmination of an ongoing and evolving process of revelation in the here and now.

The Mishnah is Judaism's counterpart to Plato's *Republic* and Aristotle's *Politics*, a noble theory of it all. When we study the Mishnah, we contemplate a fine conception of nowhere in particular, addressed to

1

whom it may concern. When we turn to the Yerushalmi, we see a
familiar world, as we have known it from then until now. We perceive
something of our own day, as we who study Judaism recognize continuity with those times. As the Mishnah marks the end of the ancient
and Near Eastern, so does the Yerushalmi the beginning of the modern
and the Western (as well as the Near Eastern) epoch in the history of
Judaism. That is why the Talmud of the Land of Israel deserves attention, in the setting not only of the history of Judaism but also of the
formation of the civilization of the West.

Let me first define the terms at hand, beginning with Judaism. The
Talmud of the Land of Israel testifies to the formation of the kind of
Judaism paramount and normative from its time to this day. Called
"Rabbinic," because of the honorific title of its principal authority, the
rabbi, or Talmudic, because of the main document on which it is based,
this particular version of Judaism proved lasting beyond its formative
years. So at issue is a moment in the birth of Judaism.

As to the time, the period is marked off at the beginning by the
completion of the Mishnah, at c. 200 C.E., and at the end by the closure of
the Talmud of the Land of Israel, at c. 400 C.E. These tumultuous
centuries witnessed the transition from late antiquity to earlier medieval
times. The Roman Empire split, dividing east from west, turning from
pagan to Christian, from the classical mode to the one we identify as
medieval. The birth of Judaism thus forms a chapter in the history of the
movement of the West from its Greek, Roman, and Israelite beginnings,
to its full expression in Christianity, for the generality of Europe: (later
on) in Islam, and for Africa and Asia. True, the birth of Judaism in
context fills little more than a paragraph out of the long chapter of the
movement from classical to medieval civilization, both east and west. But
in the end it may prove a suggestive chapter, exemplifying in its accessi-
bility much that may otherwise lie beyond our capacity for detailed
description and explanation. In what is small we may discern large
things, in detail, the configuration of the whole.

Let us now come to define what changes mark the turning of the
way. It is evoked, in literary terms, in the transition from the Mishnah to
the Talmud of the Land of Israel. As I have said, from the strict and
formal classicism of the Mishnah, like Plato's *Republic*, describing for no
one in particular an ideal society never to be seen in its day, the Judaism
described by the Talmud of the Land of Israel turned to the disorderly
detail of the workaday world, taking the utopian Mishnah along. If
Aristotle's *Politics* had been written as a gloss to Plato's *Republic*,
amplifying and extending piece by piece the once whole but no longer

cogent writing of Plato, we should have a rough analogy to what the Yerushalmi does with the Mishnah of Judah the Patriarch (henceforward: Rabbi). If, further, many philosophers took up the fantastic account of the *Republic* and out of its materials and other writings worked out new *Republics*, so bringing diversity to what had been a single conception and book, we should find a possible precedent for what happened from 200 to 400 C.E. in the move, in Judaism, from the ancient to the medieval mode: theoretical to practical, monotheistic to polytheistic, uniform to diverse, cogent to chaotic, and systematic to traditional.

The second century yielded a single document of Judaism, the Mishnah. The dawn of the fifth century witnessed the beginnings and formation of many documents, and the completion of one, this Talmud. For by that time, the Talmud of the Land of Israel, a vast amplification of the Mishnah, neared closure. Tosefta, a supplement to the Mishnah's materials in the Mishnah's own idiom and structure, was taking shape. *Sifra*, a compilation of exegeses pertinent to Leviticus, with special interest in the relationship of the Mishnah's laws to those of Leviticus, would soon follow. In the hundred years beyond the closure of the Yerushalmi, a quite different mode of collection and organization of sayings, represented by the compilations of exegetical remarks on Genesis and Leviticus called Genesis *Rabbah* and Leviticus *Rabbah*, would come to full expression. But we shouldn't silently pass by the other Talmud, the one created in Babylonia, generally thought to have come to its final condition in the two centuries after the Yerushalmi's closure. Accordingly, the Mishnah, a single document, stands at the head of many paths. Numerous roads lead forward, out of the Mishnah, but only one leads back from it—the leap from the Mishnah to Sinai, accomplished through promiscuous citing of proof-texts of Scripture. Among these paths from the Mishnah, the Palestinian and the Babylonian Talmuds mark the principal ways forward.

The Talmud of the Land of Israel testifies to the existence of a coherent worldview and way of life embodied in a distinct and distinctive society, or estate, of Jews: the rabbis—masters and disciples—of the third and fourth century in the Land of Israel. Before us in the Yerushalmi is not a complete system of Judaism, contained in a single document. The Yerushalmi is not like the Mishnah, which provides a full and exhaustive account of its system and its viewpoint. Whatever we know about the Mishnah's system is in that book itself. The Judaism to which the Yerushalmi testifies defines the matrix in which, among other documents, the Yerushalmi came into being. But the Yerushalmi does not constitute the sole important corpus of evidence about that kind of Judaism. Nor is there a single document that expresses that whole.

In this regard as in many other ways, the Yerushalmi and the Mishnah are really not comparable to one another. The Yerushalmi is continuous with the Mishnah. But the character of the document, and therefore the world to which its evidence pertains, presents us with a mirror image of the Mishnah. The first and most important difference, as already stated, is simply that the Mishnah, brought to closure at c. 200, constitutes the only document deriving from the period in which it took shape. By contrast, materials of the Yerushalmi often intersect with materials in other such documents, such as Tosefta and the Babylonian Talmud. For the Mishnah, the sole point of intersection is with the Tosefta, but that compilation is demonstrably later than the Mishnah and dependent upon it for structure, for organization, for style, and for subject matter. Accordingly, the Judaism in the Talmud of the Land of Israel is not the Judaism only of that book, in the same way in which the Judaism to which the Mishnah testifies is, expressed within the Mishnah, whole and complete.

While the Mishnah exhaustively answers any and all questions about its Judaism, the Yerushalmi, answering many questions about the Judaism represented in its pages, is by no means the only source of answers. Numerous questions, dealt with by the Judaism to which Yerushalmi attests, are answered—in the same or similar ways—in other documents altogether. The evidence of the Yerushalmi about the Judaism attested in its pages must be described in a way quite different from the way in which we lay out evidence of the Mishnah about the Judaism expressed within the Mishnah. I refer to my *Judaism: The Evidence of the Mishnah* (1981). So the one gives evidence of a world beyond itself, a world of which it is an important component. The other gives evidence only about itself and the worldview contemplated within its words.

The question now arises, how shall we make use of the evidence presented by a single, vast book—thirty-nine tractates—in describing and interpreting the religious system partially contained within that book? It seems to me the sole valid route is by providing an ample selection of the evidence. But I should have also to claim that that selection typifies the entire corpus, of which it is a mere sample. The latter claim is critical. If we deal with a mass of discrete evidence, not one item bearing any points of comparison with any other item, then the description of the religion of the book depends solely upon translating and interpreting the book. No further work is possible. Accordingly, systematic description depends upon the allegation that extracts of texts serve to exemplify the traits of many other texts in the document as a whole. They must be made to constitute, in selection and arrangement, a sustained argument. What we learn permits us to describe as a whole that part of the rabbinic system of which the Yerushalmi constitutes a principal component.

The justification for this procedure is that the Yerushalmi is a remarkably uniform document. As I shall explain in Chapter 1, the Yerushalmi speaks about many things but with a single voice. Its modes of discourse are not greatly differentiated, in particular, when any given passage of the Mishnah comes under analysis. Then we find a limited range of repetitious rhetoric of patterns through which any passage of Mishnah-exegesis will unfold.

In my translation of the Yerushalmi, *The Talmud of the Land of Israel: 35, Introduction, Taxonomy* (1982), I have already shown the remarkably limited repertoire of conceptual-exegetical initiatives available to the framers of the Yerushalmi's discussions of passages of the Mishnah. They are likely to carry out one of only a handful of procedures, and these may be reduced to two: to explain the simple meaning of a passage or to expand and theorize about one passage in the light of other passages (or of a problem common to several passages). Exegesis may therefore take the form of 1. an explanation of the meaning, or 2. an expansion upon the meaning, of a given passage. It follows that if we understand what the Talmud does with a single passage of the Mishnah, we also may confidently claim we can make sense of, and describe what the Yerushalmi is apt to do with, a great many such passages. Citation and analysis of a few passages, claimed to be representative, therefore allow the description of the mode of exegetical thought of the framers of the Yerushalmi in general. Illustrative texts illustrate because they are typical and so exemplify traits of the document as a whole. At the end I should have to provide not a few snippets, an anthology of this and that, but a complete account of the system of the document as a whole, as seen through representative and important passages illustrative of its definitive conceptual characteristics.

In identifying the Yerushalmi's evidence with the period in which the document took shape and reached closure, I listen to the single voice of the Yerushalmi. But why not ask the Yerushalmi to tell us about the period prior to 300-400 C.E., when it is generally assumed the document was written? The reason is that we cannot show that the materials testify to a period prior to that of its formation and redaction. What we cannot show we do not know, so we listen to the Yerushalmi's message in the setting of the world to which that message was addressed. We do not assume that the message took shape only in that period; our sole assumption is that the message was found cogent and relevant in that period in particular, even while components of the same message may have been worked out after 200, the closure of the Mishnah, but prior to 300. This procedure differs from the one that characterizes my reading of the formation of the system of Judaism expressed in the Mishnah, and I will explain the difference.

When I took up the study of the Mishnah, I found it possible to trace the history of some of its ideas back from the point of closure in c. 200 C.E. to their starting point nearly two centuries earlier. Accordingly, for the Mishnah's system of Judaism, it was possible to relate some sizable part of the end product to conditions prevailing prior to the closure and redaction of that end product. Specifically, I claimed to relate some of the Mishnah's laws and ideas to the period before the destruction of the Temple in 70 C.E., to the period between that event and the Bar Kochba revolt three generations later, and, finally, from the end of that war to the completion of the Mishnah itself. The reason is that the Mishnah is so laid out as to make possible the study of sequences of ideas. The tractates are internally cogent and carefully laid out. There is little overlap among them.

The Yerushalmi's layout is quite different, because it is suspended from various particles—brief declarative units—of the Mishnah, having no inner coherence whatsoever. It is exceedingly difficult systematically and comprehensively to demonstrate that any statements in the names of the authorities of the Yerushalmi testify to conditions prior to the point of closure of the document as a whole. While a few initiatives, not yet attempted, seem promising, in the main, the encompassing and systematic work done on the Mishnah—I stress, possibly because of its very character—as yet has not been attempted on the Yerushalmi.

Furthermore, I do not regard the labor as promising. Should the work flourish and we discover ways of determining which attributions are more reliable and which are less, our gain would be minimal. So much of the Yerushalmi—I estimate 90 percent—consists of close exegesis of the Mishnah itself, that the bulk of the result, for history of ideas of Judaism, would be of only modest interest. That is, I cannot think why it matters to know much about the sequential unfolding—the history—of the exegesis of the various discrete passages of the Mishnah, unless we are able to determine, also, that factors quite remote from the inner tensions and logic of the passages of the Mishnah have come into play. If I am able to relate Mishnah-exegesis to the circumstance in which the exegesis is carried out (content to context), then the work may prove suggestive beyond itself. If not, the work seems to me arid and merely academic, an exercise in cultic antiquarianism best left to people for whom the reward is self-evidently supernatural.

I wish to dwell on this matter, because my negative judgment determines my strategy for working out a picture of the Yerushalmi's Judaism, so different from the one I followed to gain a picture of the Mishnah's Judaism. To begin with, the character of the evidence has to be made clear.

The Talmud of the Land of Israel consists of passages of the Mishnah, each followed by two or more units of discourse (complete and cogent discussions of a single theme or problem) generally pertinent to that passage. These units of discourse had taken shape prior to their construction as the Yerushalmi as we know it. The work of closure and redaction was separate from the work of formulation of the several units of discourse. The units themselves, moreover, normally are made up of a conglomerate of materials. These originated in diverse ways, in that various names will be associated with the sayings at hand. The unsolved problem, as I have said, is how to come to an assessment of the ways in which the components of the Talmud of the Land of Israel may serve to describe the period from the closure of the Mishnah, in c. 200 C.E., prior to the age of the conclusion of the Yerushalmi, in c. 350-400 C.E. So the particular problem at hand is to find out how, if at all, we may learn from the Yerushalmi about the period from 200 to 350 C.E.

The evidence awaiting analysis has to be specified. Specifically, what basis do we have to suppose that anything in the Talmud Yerushalmi testifies to the state of affairs prior to redaction? The answer is simple. Numerous sayings in the Yerushalmi come to us over the names of sages alleged to have composed them or to have endorsed the views contained in them. There are, moreover, numerous allusions, throughout the Yerushalmi, to what various authorities said and did. It would be difficult to point to more than a handful of units of discourse in the entire Yerushalmi in which we do not find names of sages who are assumed to have flourished between the time of the closure of the Mishnah and that of the conclusion of the Yerushalmi. These clearly are supposed to attest to the existence and authority of the materials in which the names occur, especially where what is attributed to a given sage takes account of completed discourse before us and comments upon it. So the question of treating the Yerushalmi as a corpus of information on a period prior to that of its own closure depends upon the simple fact that most of the units of discourse are assigned to specific, named authorities. Without those names nothing is possible.

Short of simply accepting the accuracy of these attributions and so assuming that if the Yerushalmi says Rabbi X made a statement, he really *did* make it, we must construct a mode of evaluating these data—

the available names and sayings. First, are there truly reliable ways by which we may test the allegation that a given saying really was said by the authority to whom it is assigned? The answer is that there surely are, but we simply do not have them. If we had not only the Yerushalmi, with its third-person references to rabbis, but also writings, compiled and preserved by a given rabbi in his own hand or among his own disciples, we might then test the allegation of the Yerushalmi. We should know how to sort out the valid from the pseudepigraphic attributions, verifying the one, falsifying the other. But the only evidence we have about the rabbis of the Yerushalmi—a collective, anonymous document—is what the Yerushalmi itself tells us. There is nothing personal; there is nothing outside of the document itself. Accordingly, we have no way whatsoever of investigating whether a given rabbi really said what was attributed to him.

If we do not know whether a rabbi really said what is attributed to him, then what do we learn from the fact that the name of someone assumed to have flourished at a certain time is attached to a specific saying or story? It is the indisputable but paltry fact that someone, sometime after that named authority, assumed and persuaded others to believe that said rabbi *had* said or done what that sage, in succession, alleged. On the face of it, then, we may state the Yerushalmi's historical claim very simply. We can never assess the facts of the matter. We do have the fact that someone believed and transmitted as authoritative the stated allegation as the facts of the matter. This historical claim is somewhat different from the one we have set aside. That is, we do not know that Rabbi X said or did what is alleged, but we do know that someone at some point thereafter—a day? a century?—believed that he had said and done it.

The criteria, suited to internal evidence, by which we may test the historical allegations at hand—that is to say, the claim that we may differentiate among sayings and assign some to an earlier, others to a later, period—have now to be specified, then themselves assessed. What criteria are these?

1. **Adherence to intelligible criteria, consistently revealed:** In evaluating the policies behind assigning sayings to a given name, the first question must be whether or not the practice is consistent or capricious. If we are able to show that a cogent set of principles is associated with a given name, then we have reason to claim to validate or deny the attribution, to that name, of opinions on diverse subjects pertinent to a single principle. On such a basis, we may show that a given saying either is, or is not, consistent with others by that same name. The upshot is the

possibility of demonstrating that an intelligible and coherent set of reasons stands behind the use of names for the differentiation of sayings.

2. Progression of principles from simpler and more fundamental to more complex and derivative, parallel with succession of authorities from an earlier to a later generation: Alongside the issue of consistency of what is assigned to a given name comes a second consideration. If what is assigned to an early authority takes for granted issues or facts otherwise attested only in the name of several later authorities, then on the face of it the assignment in the former instance is dubious. Since we cannot imagine we deal with prophets, we have to suppose that what is attributed to the earlier authority, incomprehensible except in light of what is otherwise known only in the mouths of later authorities, is in fact pseudepigraphic. Here too there is the possibility of verifying or falsifying attributions.

If these two criteria were to be systematically applied, we should have some slight basis on which to estimate how the Yerushalmi may serve for historical purposes. That is to say, we might then interpret the implications of the Yerushalmi's consistency in its views of what a given authority had said, of the movement of discourse from primitive to more sophisticated in close tandem with the movement of the period of the sages to whom discourse is assigned from earlier to later times. On this basis a history of the ideas of the document might come into view. What sort of ideas might then be shown to have a history? Since the bulk of the document provides ad hoc and episodic observations about the meaning of a brief passage of the Mishnah, the upshot would be tiny histories indeed, sherds and remnants of thousands of jugs from how many potteries we do not know. No one would maintain that the work of analysis of the literary and conceptual traits of the document, leading to a picture of which passages come first, which come later on, is without promise. On the contrary, a more sophisticated grasp of how the document came into being and the relationship between what people really said and did and what the Yerushalmi's framers claim they said and did will open many paths of inquiry and interpretation. But, as always, the best is the enemy of the good. This far we can now go. Now to the document itself.

1

The Yerushalmi as Literature: Many Voices, One Melody

When we speak of "the Yerushalmi," it is because the document, while drawing on a variety of voices, presents a single melody. To appreciate what that means, we must remember that the Yerushalmi is broken up into multiple brief discourses, discussions of the meaning and sense of the phrases and sentences of the Mishnah. Nearly every discourse—perhaps 90 percent of the whole—of the Yerushalmi addresses one main point: the meaning of the Mishnah. For the Yerushalmi, the life of Israel reaches the level of analysis within the integument of the Mishnah. That is to say, the Mishnah is about life, while the Yerushalmi is about the Mishnah. Accordingly, the traits of the Mishnah defined the problematic areas of both intellect and politics, confronting the heirs of the Mishnah, the disciples of the final generation of the Mishnah's redaction and formulation. They, for their part, set the patterns that followed, treating the Mishnah as Torah, proposing to receive and realize its revelation. But then how can people make a statement of their own, when their focus is upon statements of others, prior to themselves?

The reason is simple. The Yerushalmi speaks about the Mishnah in essentially a single voice, about fundamentally few things. Its mode of speech and thought is uniform throughout. Diverse topics produce slight differentiation in modes of analysis. The same sorts of questions phrased in the same rhetoric—a moving, or dialectical, argument, composed of questions and answers—turn out to pertain equally well to every passage of the Mishnah. It generally takes up a single, not very complex or diverse, program of inquiry. The Yerushalmi also utilizes a single, rather

11

limited repertoire of exegetical initiatives and rhetorical choices for whatever discourse about the Mishnah the framers propose to undertake. Accordingly, as is clear, the Yerushalmi presents us with both a uniformity of discourse and a monotony of tone. The Yerushalmi speaks in a single voice. That voice by definition is collective, not greatly differentiated by traits of individuals. Individuals in the Yerushalmi, unlike in the Mishnah, do not speak uniformly, but the differences are not marked. Let me spell this out, because its consequences for the history of the ideas contained within Yerushalmi will prove definitive.

The Yerushalmi identifies no author or collegium of authors. When I say that the Yerushalmi speaks in a single voice, I mean to say that it speaks uniformly, consistently, and predictably. The voice is the voice of a book, the voice of an author, the voice we hear when we read: one voice. The message is one deriving from a community, the collectivity of sages or textual community for whom and to whom the book speaks. The document seems, in the main, to intend to provide notes, an abbreviated script that anyone may use to reconstruct and reenact formal discussions of problems: about *this*, one says *that*. Curt and often arcane, these notes can be translated only with immense bodies of inserted explanation. All of this script of information is public and undifferentiated, not individual and idiosyncratic. We must assume people took for granted that, out of the signs of speech, it would be possible for anyone to reconstruct speech, doing so in accurate and fully conventional ways. So the literary traits of the document presuppose a uniform code of communication: a single voice.

THE ORIGINS

The ubiquitous character of this single and continuous voice of the Yerushalmi argues for one of two points of origin. First, powerful and prevailing conventions may have been formed in the earliest stages of the reception and study of the Mishnah, then carried on thereafter without variation or revision. Or, second, the framing of sayings into uniform constructions of discourse may have been accomplished only toward the end of the period marked by the formation of the Yerushalmi's units of discourse and their conglomeration into the Yerushalmi of the Land of Israel as we know it.

In the former case, we posit that the mode of reasoned analysis of the Mishnah and the repertoire of issues to be addressed to any passage of the Mishnah were defined early on, then persisted for two hundred years. The consequent, conventional mode of speech yielded that nearly total uniformity of discourse characteristic of numerous units of discourse of the Yerushalmi at which the interpretation of a law of the Mishnah is subject to discussion. In the latter case we surmise that a vast corpus of sayings, some by themselves, some parts of larger conglomerates, was inherited at some point toward the end of the two hundred years under discussion. This corpus of miscellanies was then subjected to intense consideration as a whole, shaped and reworded into the single, cogent, and rhetorically consistent Yerushalmiic discourse before us.

Of these two possibilities, the latter seems by far the more likely. The reason is simple. I cannot find among the units of discourse in the Mishnah evidence of differentiation among the generations of names or schools. There is no interest, for instance, in the chronological sequence in which sayings took shape and in which discussions may be supposed to have taken place. That is to say, the Yerushalmiic unit of discourse approaches the explanation of a passage of the Mishnah without systematic attention to the layers in which ideas were set forth, the schools among which discussion must have been divided, the sequence in which statements about a Mishnah-law were made. That fact points to formation at the end, not agglutination in successive layers of intellectual sediment. Let me spell this out. In a given unit of discourse, the focus, the organizing principle, the generative interest—are defined solely by the issue at hand. The argument moves from point to point, directed by the inner logic of argument itself. A single plane of discourse is established. All things are leveled out, so that the line of logic runs straight and true. Accordingly, a single conception of the framing and formation of the unit of discourse stands prior to the spelling out of issues. More fundamental still, what people in general wanted was not to create topical anthologies—to put together instances of what this one said about that issue—but to exhibit the logic of that issue, viewed under the aspect of eternity. Under sustained inquiry we always find a theoretical issue, freed of all temporal considerations and the contingencies of politics and circumstance.

Once these elemental literary facts make their full impression on our understanding, everything else falls into place as well. Arguments such as the ones we shall now review did not unfold over a long period of time, as one generation made its points, to be followed by the additions and revisions of another generation, in a process of gradual increment and agglutination running on for two hundred years. That theory of the formation of literature cannot account for the unity, stunning force and dynamism, of the Yerushalmi's dialectical arguments. To the contrary, someone (or small group) at the end determined to reconstruct, so as to expose, the naked logic of a problem. For this purpose, oftentimes, it was found useful to cite sayings or positions from earlier times. But these inherited materials underwent a process of reshaping, and, more aptly, refocusing. Whatever the original words—and we need not doubt that at times we have them—the point of everything in hand was defined and determined by the people who made it all up at the end. The whole shows a plan and program. It is not that the principles of chronology were wholly ignored. Rather, they were not determinative of the structure of argument. So I do not suggest that the framers of the Yerushalmi would likely have an early authority argue with a later one about what is assigned only to the later one. That I cannot and do not expect to instantiate. I do not think we shall find such slovenly work in either our Yerushalmi or the other one. Our sages were painstaking and sensible. The point is that no attention is ever devoted in particular to the sequence in which various things are said. Everything is worked together into a single, temporally seamless discourse. Thus, if a unit of discourse draws upon ideas of authorities of the first half of the third century, such as Simeon b. Laqish and Yohanan, as well as those of figures of the second half of the fourth century, such as Yose, Jonah, Huna, Zeira, and Yudan, while discourse will be continuous, discussion will always focus upon the logical point at hand.

It follows that the whole is the work of the one who decided to make up the discussion on the atemporal logic of the point at issue. Otherwise the discussion would not be continuous but disjointed, full of seams and margins, marks of the existence of prior conglomerations of materials that have now been sewn together. What we have are not patchwork quilts, but woven fabric. Along these lines, we may find discussions in which opinions of Palestinians, such as Yohanan and Simeon b. Laqish, will be joined together side by side with opinions of Babylonians, such as Rab and Samuel. The whole, once again, will unfold in a smooth way, so that the issues at hand define the sole focus of discourse. The logic of those issues will be fully exposed. Considerations of the origin of a saying in one country or the other will play no role whatsoever in the rhetoric or literary forms of argument. There will be no possibility of differentiation among opinions on the basis of where, when, by whom, or how they are formulated, only on the basis of what, in fact, is said.

THE CONSTRUCTION

In my view it follows that the whole—the unit of discourse as we know it—was put together at the end. At that point everything was in hand, so available for arrangement in accordance with a principle other than chronology, and in a rhetoric common to all sayings. That other principle will then have determined the arrangement, drawing in its wake a resort to a single monotonous voice: "the Yerushalmi." The principle is logical exposition, that is to say, the analysis and dissection of a problem into its conceptual components. The dialectic of argument is framed not by considerations of the chronological sequence in which sayings were said but by attention to the requirements of reasonable exposition of the problem. That is what governs.

We know that the Mishnah was formulated in its rigid, patterned language and carefully organized and enumerated groups of formal-substantive cognitive units, in the very processes in which it also was redacted. Otherwise the correspondences between redactional program and formal and patterned mode of articulation of ideas cannot be explained, short of invoking the notion of a literary miracle. The Yerushalmi evidently underwent a process of redaction, in which fixed and final units of discourse (whether as I have delineated them or in some other division) were organized and put together. The most likely antecedent work of framing and formulating these units of discourse appears to have gone on in a single period. By this I mean, among a relatively small number of sages working within a uniform set of literary conventions at roughly the same time, and in approximately the same way. These framers of the various units of tradition may or may not have participated in the work of closure and redaction of the whole. We do not know the answer. But among themselves they cannot have differed very much about the way in which the work was to be carried on. For the end product, the Yerushalmi, like the Mishnah, is uniform and stylistically coherent, generally consistent in modes of thought and speech, wherever we turn. That accounts for the single voice that leads us through the dialectical and argumentative analysis of the Yerushalmi. That voice is ubiquitous and insistent. Let us now listen to it.

We begin with a set of instances that illustrate the fundamental traits of discourse. What we see is that the discussion is coherent and harmonious, moving from beginning to what was, in fact, a predetermined end. The voice of the Yerushalmi speaks to us throughout, not the diverse voices of real people engaged in a concrete and therefore chaotic argument, but as in Plato's dialogues, question and answer—the dialectical argument—which constitutes conventions through which logic is exposed and tested, not the reports of things people said spontaneously or even after the fact. The controlling voice is monotonous, lacking all points of differentiation of viewpoint, tone, mode of inquiry, and thought.

This is what I mean to illustrate here. To prove this same proposition incontrovertibly, I should have to cite a vast proportion of the Yerushalmi as a whole. A few instances must suffice.

THE ANALYSIS

The first example is Y. [Yerushalmi] [to Mishnah-tractate] Niddah [Chapter] 1:[Paragraph] 3. In the opening passage, the language of the Mishnah-pericope is subjected to close analysis and clarification. What is important in the three units of discourse before us is that matters are conducted so that a single voice—the Yerushalmi—leads us through the problem. Unit II is striking. Clearly, an editor has selected and inserted the passage of Tosefta cited here. We can surmise, by reference to the passage of the Mishnah under discussion, why the passage seemed important. The discourse takes place on a single plane, established and defined solely by the logic at hand. The use of question and answer is artifice, and does not indicate an actual conversation. I give the Mishnah-passage in boldface type.

> A. **Who is a virgin [Among the four women who fall into the category of those for whom the time of first seeing blood suffices, without scruple as to prior contamination by reason of doubt]?**
> B. **Any girl who has never in her life produced a drop of [menstrual] blood,**
> C. **even though she is married.**

> I. A. This is the teaching of the Mishnah: Any girl who has not seen menstrual blood in her life, and even though she is married.
> B. They [thus] spoke of a virgin as to blood, [that is, a girl who had never menstruated], not a virgin as to the hymen.
> C. There are cases in which a girl is a virgin as to blood and not a virgin as to the hymen. There are cases in which she is a virgin as to the hymen but is not a virgin as to blood.
> D. [A girl is] a virgin as to the hymen when she produced a drop of blood and afterward was married.

      E. [She is a] virgin as to blood when she was married
         and afterward produced a drop of blood.

  II. A. It was taught in a Tannaitic saying:
       **B. There are three kinds of virgins: a virgin woman, a
         virgin sycamore, and virgin soil. A virgin woman is
         any woman who has never had sexual intercourse. A
         virgin sycamore is any that has never been chopped
         down. Virgin soil is any that has never been worked.
         Rabban Simeon b. Gamaliel says, "It is any in which
         there is not a single sherd" [T. Shebiit 3:14H, 15].**

    At Y. Horayot 2:1 once again we have a sustained discussion, this
time on the exegetical foundations of a law of the Mishnah. The voice of
the Yerushalmi is undifferentiated; the entire passage concentrates on
the substance of matters. A single hand surely stands behind it all, for
there is not a single seam or margin. So to give an account of the matter,
we must speak in the name of "the Yerushalmi." That is, "the Yerushalmi" wants to know the relationship of an anointed priest to a court,
the reciprocal authority of autonomous institutions. Scripture has specified several autonomous persons and institutions or groups that atone
with a bullock for erroneous actions committed inadvertently. So the
Yerushalmi now raises the interesting question of the rule that applies
when one of these autonomous bodies follows instructions given by
another. The unit explores this question, first establishing that the
anointed priest is equivalent to the community, just as Scripture states,
and drawing the consequence of that fact. Then comes the important
point that the anointed priest is autonomous of the community. He
atones for what he does, but is not subject to atonement by, or in behalf
of, others.

      A. [If] an anointed [high] priest made a decision for
         himself [in violation of any of the commandments of
         the Torah] doing so inadvertently, and carrying out
         [his decision] inadvertently,
      B. he brings a bullock [Leviticus 4:3].
      C. [If] he [made an erroneous decision] inadvertently,
         and deliberately carried it out, or
      D. deliberately [made an erroneous decision] and inad-
         vertently carried it out,

E. he is exempt.

F. For [as to A-B] an [erroneous] decision of an anointed [high priest] for himself is tantamount to an [erroneous] decision of a court for the entire community.

I. A. ["If any one sins unwittingly in any of the things which the Lord has commanded not to be done and does any one of them, if it is the anointed priest who sins, thus bringing guilt on the people, then let him offer for the sin which he has committed a young bull" (Leviticus 4:23-30)]. "Anyone . . ." "If it is the high priest . . ."—lo, [the Scripture would seem to imply that] the high priest is tantamount to an individual [and not, vs. M. Horayot 2:1F, to an embodiment of the community and thus not subject to a bullock-offering.]

B. [In this case, Scripture's purpose is to say:] Just as an individual, if he ate [something prohibited] at the instruction of a court is exempt, so this one [subject to court authority], if he ate something at the instruction of the court, is exempt.

C. Just as an individual, if he ate [something prohibited] without the instruction of a court is liable, so this one, if he ate something not at the instruction of a court, is liable.

D. [To encounter that possible interpretation] Scripture states, "Thus bringing guilt on the people" [meaning] lo, [the high anointed priest's] guilt is tantamount to the guilt of the entire people [just as M. Horayot 2:1F states].

E. Just as the people are not guilty unless they gave instruction [Leviticus 4:13], so this one is not guilty unless he gave instruction.

F. There is a Tannaitic tradition that interprets [the matter with reference to] the people [and] the court:

G. Just as [if] the people gave instruction and other people did [what the people] said, [the people] are liable, so this one, [if] he gave [erroneous] instruction and others did [what he said], should be liable.

H. [It is to counter that possible interpretation that]

Scripture states, "[If it is the high priest] who sins," [meaning] for the sin that this one himself committed he brings [a bullock], but he does not have to bring a bullock on account of what other people do [inadvertently sinning because of his instruction].

I. There is a Tannaitic tradition that interprets the [matter with reference to] the people [and] the community:

J. Just as, in the case of the people, if others gave erroneous instruction and they [inadvertently] committed a sin, they are liable, so in the case of this one, [if] others gave erroneous instruction and he carried it out [and so sinned], he should be liable.

K. [To counter that possible, wrong interpretation,] Scripture states, "[If it is the high priest] who sins," [meaning] for the sin that this one committed, he brings [a bullock], but he does not have to bring a bullock on account of what other people do [inadvertently sinning because of their instruction].

We find at Y. Sanhedrin 4:9 a further instance in which the argument is so constructed as to speak to an issue, without regard to the source of sayings or the definition of the voices in conversation. A question is asked, then answered, because the rhetoric creates dialectic, movement from point to point. It is not because an individual speaks with, and interrogates, yet another party. The uniform voice of the Yerushalmi is before us, lacking all distinguishing traits, following a single, rather simple program of rhetorical conventions.

II. A. And perhaps you might want to claim, "What business is it of ours to convict this man of a capital crime?"[M. Sanhedrin 4:9]

B. It is written, "And about sunset a cry went through the army" (I Kings 22:36).

C. What is this cry?

D. Lo, it a song, as it is said, "When the wicked perish, there is a song" (Proverbs 11:10).

E. But, on the contrary, it also is said, "[That they should praise] as they went out before the army [and say, 'Give thanks unto the Lord, for his mercy endures for ever']" (II Chronicles 20:21).

F. [Omitting the words, 'for he is good,'] is to teach you
that even the downfall of the wicked is no joy before
the Omnipresent.

Y. Makkot 1:5 presents yet another example in which a sustained
conversation on a passage of Scripture, unfolding through questions and
answers, conforms to a simple rhetorical program. The voice of the
interlocutor is not differentiated from the source of the respondent, for
the whole is a single discourse. Not a "real" conversation, but rather an
effective presentation of a simple idea.

I. A. [Scripture refers to the requirement of two or three
witnesses to impose the death penalty (Deuteronomy
17:6). Scripture further states, "Only on the evidence
of two witnesses or of three witnesses shall a charge
be sustained" (Deuteronomy 19:15). The former deals
with capital cases, the latter with property cases.
Since both refer to two or three witnesses, the dupli-
cation is now explained:] Scripture is required to refer
to property cases, and also to capital cases.

B. For if it had referred to property cases and not to
capital cases, I might have said, in the case of property
cases, which are of lesser weight, three witnesses have
the power to prove two to be perjurers, but two may
not prove three to be perjurers.

C. How do I know that that is so even of a hundred?

D. Scripture states, "Witnesses."

E. Now if reference had been made to capital cases, and
not to property cases, I might have said, in capital
cases, which are weightier, two witnesses have the
power to prove that three are perjurers but three do
not have the power to prove that two are perjurers.

F. How do I know that that applies even to a hundred?

G. Scripture says, "Witnesses." [It follows then the
Scripture must refer to "two or three" in the context of
each matter, since one could not have derived the one
from the other.]

All of the units of discourse before us exhibit the same traits. In each
instance we see that the conversation is artificial. What is portrayed is
not real people but a kind of rhetoric. The presence of questions and

answers is a literary convention, not a (pretended) transcription of a conversation. So we may well speak of the Yerushalmi's voice: that is all we have. The absence of differentiation is not the sole striking trait. We observe, also, a well-planned and pointed program of inquiry, however brief, leading to a single purpose for each unit of discourse. While the various units in theme are completely unrelated to one another, in rhetoric and mode of analysis they are essentially uniform: simple questions, simple answers, uncomplex propositions, worked out through reference to authoritative sources of law, essentially an unfolding of information.

In these passages the Yerushalmi takes on its own timeless voice. But how does it deal with passages in which there are named authorities? These, on the surface, testify to specific periods in the two centuries at hand, since the authorities mentioned lived at specific times and places. If, now, we observe the same uniformity of tone and dialectic, we shall address a somewhat more refined problem. The important point in the examples that follow is that while named authorities and sayings assigned to them do occur, the dialectic of argument is conducted outside the contributions of the specified sages. Sages' statements serve the purposes of the anonymous voice, rather than defining and governing the flow of argument. So the anonymous voice, the Yerushalmi, predominates even when individuals' sayings are utilized. Selecting and arranging whatever was in hand is the work of one hand, one voice.

What is interesting at Y. Abodah Zarah 1:5, an account of the language of the Mishnah, is that the framer of the entire discussion takes over and uses what is attributed to Hiyya. The passage requires Hiyya's version of the Mishnah-rule. But Hiyya is not responsible for the formation of the passage. It is the Yerushalmi that speaks, drawing upon the information, including the name, of Hiyya. Only the secondary comment in the name of Bun bar Hiyya violates the monotone established by the Yerushalmi. And at the end that same voice takes over and draws matters to their conclusion, a phenomenon we shall shortly see again. It is not uncommon for later fourth-century names to occur in such a setting.

A. **These are things [which it is] forbidden to sell to Gentiles:**

B. **(1) fir cones, (2) white figs, (3) and their stalks, (4) frankincense, and (5) a white cock.**

A. We repeat in the Mishnah-pericope [the version]: A white cock.

B. R. Hiyya repeated [for his version of] the Mishnah-pericope: "A cock of any sort."

C. The present version of the Mishnah [specifying a white cock] requires also the version of R. Hiyya, and the version of R. Hiyya requires also the [present] version of the Mishnah.

D. [Why both?] If we repeated [the present version of the Mishnah], and we did not repeat the version of R. Hiyya, we should have reached the conclusion that the sages state the rule only in regard to a white cock, but as to any sort of cock other than that, even if this was all by itself [M. Abodah Zarah 1:5D], it is permitted. Thus there was need for the Mishnah-version of R. Hiyya.

E. Now if one repeated the version of R. Hiyya, and we did not repeat the version before us in the Mishnah, we should have ruled that the rule applies only in the case of an unspecified cock [requested by the purchaser], but [if the purchaser requested] a white cock, then even if this was all by itself, it would be prohibited [to sell such a cock].

F. Thus there was need for the Mishnah-version as it is repeated before us, and there also was need for the Mishnah-version as it is repeated by R. Hiyya.

G. Said R. Bun bar Hiyya, "[In Hiyya's view, if a Gentile said, 'Who has] a cock to sell?' one may sell him a white cock, [so Hiyya differs from, and does not merely complement, the version of the Mishnah-pericope]."

H. [Now if the Gentile should say, "Who has] a white cock to sell," we then rule that if the white cock is by itself, it is forbidden, but if it is part of a flock of cocks, it is permitted to sell it to him. [This clearly is the position of the Mishnah-pericope, so there is no dispute at all, merely complementary traditions, as argued at D–E.]

Here at Y. Shebuot 3:7 is yet another instance, but a more complex and better articulated one, in which topically interesting sayings attributed to two principal authorities, Yohanan and Simeon b. Laqish, provide a pretext for a rather elaborate discussion. A discussion is conducted about what Yohanan and Simeon are supposed to have said. But the rhetoric is such that they are not presented as the active voices. Their views are described. But they, personally and individually, do not express views. Predictably, the language in no way differentiates between Yohanan's and Simeon b. Laqish's manner of speech. Only the substance of what is said tells us how and about what they differ. The reason is obvious. The focus of discourse is the principle at hand, the logic to be analyzed and fully spelled out. The uniform voice of the Yerushalmi speaks throughout.

A. "I swear that I won't eat this loaf of bread," "I swear that I won't eat it," "I swear that I won't eat it"—
B. and he ate it—
C. he is liable on only one count.
D. This is a "rash oath" (Leviticus 5:4).
E. On account of deliberately [taking a rash oath] one is liable to flogging, and on account of inadvertently [taking a rash oath] he is liable to an offering of variable value.

I. A. [If someone said], "I swear that I shall eat this loaf of bread today," and the day passed, but then he ate it—
B. R. Yohanan and R. Simeon b. Laqish—both of them say, "He is exempt [from flogging for deliberate failure]."
C. The reason for the position of one authority is not the same as the reason for the ruling of the other.
D. The reason for the ruling of R. Yohanan is on the grounds that the case is one in which there can be no appropriate warning [that what the man is about to do will violate the law, because the warning can come only too late, when the day has already passed].
E. The reason for the ruling, in R. Simeon b. Laqish's view, is that [by not eating] the man is thereby violating a negative rule which does not involve an actual, concrete deed.
F. What is the practical difference between the positions of the two authorities?
G. A case in which he burned the bread and threw it into the sea.
H. If you say that the reason is on the count that the man

is not in a position to receive a warning, the man will be exempt [on the same grounds in the present case].

I. But if you say that the reason is that the matter involves a negative commandment in which there is no concrete deed, here we do have a concrete deed [namely, throwing the bread into the sea].

At Y. Shebuot 3:9 we have a still more striking instance in which the entire focus of discourse is the logic. No rhetorical devices distinguish one party to the argument from the other. The two speak in rigidly patterned language, so that what is assigned to the one always constitutes a mirror image of what is assigned to the other. That the whole, in fact, merely refers to positions taken by each is clear in the resort to third person and descriptive language, in place of the attributive, "said."

A. "I swear that I shall eat this loaf of bread," "I swear that I shall not eat it"—the first statement is a rash oath, and the second is a vain oath [M. Shebuot 3:9A-B].

B. How do they treat such a case [in which a man has taken these contradictory oaths, one of which he must violate]?

C. They instruct him to eat [the loaf].

D. It is better to transgress a vain oath and not to transgress a rash oath.

E. "I swear that I shall not eat this loaf of bread," "I swear that I shall eat it"—the first is a rash oath, the second a vain oath.

F. How do they treat such a case?

G. They instruct him not to eat it.

H. It is better to transgress a vain oath by itself, and not to transgress both a vain oath and a rash oath.

I. "I swear that I shall eat this loaf of bread today," "I swear that I shall not eat it today," and he ate it—

J. R. Yohanan said, "He has carried out the first oath and nullified the second."

K. R. Simeon b. Laqish said, "He has nullified the first and not carried out the second."

L. "I swear that I shall not eat this loaf of bread today," "I swear that I shall eat it today," and he ate it—

M. R. Yohanan said, "He has nullified the first oath and carried out the second."

N. R. Simeon b. Laqish said, "He has nullified the first oath and as to the second, they instruct him to carry it out with another loaf of bread."

O. "I swear that I shall eat this loaf today," "I swear that I shall eat it today," and he ate it—

P. R. Yohanan said, "He has carried out both oaths."

Q. And R. Simeon b. Laqish said, "He has carried out the first, and as to the second, they instruct him to carry it out with another loaf of bread."

R. "I swear that I shall not eat this loaf of bread," "I swear that I shall not eat it today," and he ate it—

S. in the view of R. Yohanan, he is liable on only one count.

T. In the view of R. Simeon b. Laqish, is he liable on two counts?

U. [No.] Even R. Simeon b. Laqish will concede that he [has repeated himself] because he merely [wishes to] keep himself away from prohibited matters [and that is why he repeated the oath, but only one count is at hand].

The final, Y. Sanhedrin 5:2, example does utilize the attributive, with the implication that we have an effort to represent not merely the gist of an authority's opinion, but his exact words. Even if we assume that before us are *ipsissima verba* (the exact words) of Rab and Yohanan, however, we have still to concede the paramount role of the Yerushalmi in the formation and unpacking of the argument. For, as we notice, as soon as Rab and Yohanan have spoken, curiously mirroring one another's phrasing and wording, the monotonous voice takes over. At that point, the argument unfolds in a set of questions and answers, the standard dialectic thus predominating once again. The secondary expansion of the matter, beginning at O, then adduces a piece of evidence, followed by an anonymous discourse in which that evidence is absorbed into, and made to serve, the purposes of the analysis as a whole. Once more the fact that each item is balanced by the next is not the important point, though it is striking. What is important is that movement of the argument is defined by the Yerushalmi, and not by the constituents of discourse given in the names of specific authorities. The mind and voice behind the whole are not Rab's and Yohanan's, or, so far as we can see, their immediate disciples'. The voice is the Yerushalmi's, which does not tire, as its tertiary explication, testing the views of each and showing the full extent of the position taken by both principal parties, runs on and on. Only at the end, with Mana and Abin, fourth-century figures, do named authorities intervene in such a way as to break the uniform rhetorical pattern established.

A. There we learned:

B. He concerning whom two groups of witnesses gave testimony—

C. these testify that he took a vow to be a Nazir for two spells,

D. and those testify that he took a vow to be Nazir for five spells—

E. The House of Shammai say, "The testimony is at variance, and no Naziriteship applies here at all."

F. And the House of Hillel say, "In the sum of five are two spells, so let him serve out two spells of Naziriteship" [M. Nazir 3:7].

G. Rab said, "As to a general number [the Houses] are in disagreement [that is, as to whether he has taken the Nazirite vow at all]. But as to a specific number, all parties agree that [the testimony is at variance].

H. R. Yohanan said, "As to spelling out the number of vows there is a difference of opinion, but as to a general number, all parties concur that [within the general principle of five spells of Naziriteship there are two upon which all parties concur]. [The testimony is at variance.]"

I. What is meant by the "general number," and what is meant by "counting out the number of specific vows" [the man is supposed to have taken]? [Examples of each are as follows:]

J. The general number—one party has said, "Two," and one party has said, "Five."

K. Counting out the number of vows one by one is when one said "One, two," and the other said, "Three, four."

L. Rab said, "If the essence of the testimony is contradicted, the testimony is not null."

M. And R. Yohanan said, "If the essence of the testimony is contradicted, the testimony is null."

N. All parties concede, however, [that] if testimony has been contradicted in its nonessentials, the testimony [of the first set of witnesses] is not nullified.

O. The full extent of the position taken by R. Yohanan is seen in the following case:

P. For R. Bun bar Hiyya in the name of R. Yohanan: "The assumption [that a loan has taken place is] confirmed [by testimony] that one has counted out [coins].

Q. "If this witness says, 'From his pocket did he count out the money,' and that one says, 'From his pouch did he count out the money,'

R. "we have a case in which a testimony is contradicted in its essentials [within the same pair of witnesses, who thus do not agree]. [This testimony is null.]"

S. Here even Rab concedes that the testimony is null.

T. Concerning what do they differ?

U. Concerning a case in which there were two groups of witnesses.

V. One states, "From the pocket did he count out the money," and the other says, "From the pouch did he count out the money."

W. Here we have a case in which testimony is contradicted in its essentials. The effect of the testimony [in Yohanan's view] is null.

X. But in the view of Rab, the effect of the testimony is not null.

Y. If one witness says, "From his vest did he count out the money," and the other says, "From his wallet,"

Z. in the opinion of all parties, the testimony is contradicted in its nonessentials and therefore the testimony is not nullified. [This testimony is not about the essence of the case.]

AA. If one party says, "With a sword did he kill him," and the other party says, "With a staff did he kill him," we have a case in which testimony has been contradicted in its essentials [just as in a property case, so in a capital one].

BB. Even Rab concedes that the effect of the entire testimony is null.

CC. In what regard did they differ?

DD. In a case in which there were two sets of two witnesses:

EE. One group says, "With a sword . . ." and the other says, "With a staff . . .".

FF. Here we have a case in which the testimony has been contradicted in its essentials, and the effect of the testimony is null.

GG. But in the view of Rab, the effect of the testimony is not null.

HH. One witness says, "[The murderer] turned toward the north [to flee]," and the other witness says, "He turned toward the south," in the opinion of all parties, the testimony [of one group] has been contradicted in its nonessentials, and the testimony has not been nullified.

II. The full force of Rab's opinion is indicated in the following, which we have learned there:

JJ. [If one woman says, "He died," and one says, "He was killed," R. Meir says, "Since they contradict one another in details of their testimony, lo, these women may not remarry."] R. Judah and R. Simeon say, "Since this one and that one are in agreement that he is not alive, they may remarry" [M. Yebamot 15:5B-D].

KK. Now did he not hear that which R. Eleazar said, "R. Judah and R. Simeon concur in the matter of witnesses [that where they contradict one another in essentials, their testimony is null]?"

LL. If so, what is the difference between such contradiction when it comes from witnesses and the same when it comes from co-wives?

MM. They did not treat the statement of a co-wife concerning her fellow-wife as of any consequence whatsoever.

NN. Said R. Yohanan, "If R. Eleazar made such a statement, he heard it from me and said it."

OO. The Mishnah-pericope is at variance with the position of Rab. All the same are interrogation and examination in the following regard: When the witnesses contradict one another, their testimony is null [M. Sanhedrin 5:2F]. [Rab does not deem it invariably null, as we have seen.]

QQ. Said R. Mana, "Rab interprets the Mishnah-rule to speak of a case in which one witness contradicts another [but not in which a set of witnesses contradicts another such set in some minor detail]."

RR. Said R. Abin, "Even if you interpret the passage to speak of contradictions between one set of witnesses and another, still Rab will be able to deal with the matter. For a capital case is subject to a different rule, since it is said, 'Justice, [and only] justice, will you pursue'" (Deuteronomy 16:20). [Thus capital trials are subject to a different set of rules of evidence from those applicable in property cases, of which Rab spoke above at L.]

Since this final example is somewhat protracted, we had best review the point of citing it before we proceed. The issue of the interpretation of the passage of the Mishnah, A-F, is phrased at G-H, the conflict between Rab and Yohanan. We note that the former spent most of his mature years in Babylonia, the latter, in the Land of Israel. Accordingly, considerations of geographical or institutional relationship play no role whatsoever. The language of the one is a mirror image of what is given to the other. Then the Yerushalmi takes over, by providing an exegesis of the cited dispute, I-K. This yields a secondary phrasing of the opinions of the two authorities, L, M, with a conclusion at N. Then the position of Yohanan is provided yet a further amplification, O-R.

But what results, S, is a revision of our view of Rab's opinion. Consequently, a further exegesis of the dispute is supplied, T-U, spelled out at W-X, then with further amplication still, now at Y-BB. Once more we attempt a further account of the fundamental point at issue between the two masters, CC-HH, and, in the model of the foregoing exercise with Yohanan, Rab's view is carried to its logical extreme, II-JJ. The final part of the passage, tacked on and essentially secondary, allows for some further discussion of Rab's view, with a late authority, Mana, and his contemporary, Abin (QQ-RR) writing a conclusion to the whole. Up to that point, it seems to me clear, what we have is a rather elegant, cogent, highly stylized mode of exposition through argument, with a single form of logic applied time and again.

When I claim that the Yerushalmi's focus of interest is in the logical exposition of the law, here is a good instance of what I mean. The materials are organized so as to facilitate explanations of the law's inner structure and potentiality, not to present a mere repertoire of ideas and opinions of interest for their own sake. The upshot is a sustained argument, not an anthology of relevant sayings. Such a cogent and ongoing argument is more likely the work of a single mind than of a committee, let alone of writers who lived over a period of ten or fifteen decades.

The role of individuals in the passages we have reviewed is unimportant. The paramount voice is that of "the Yerushalmi." The rhetoric of the Yerushalmi may be described very simply: a preference for questions and answers and a willingness to test the answers and to expand them through secondary and tertiary amplification, achieved through further questions and answers. The whole gives the appearance of the script for a conversation to be reconstructed, or an argument of logical possibilities to be reenacted, in one's own mind. In this setting we of course shall be struck by the uniformity of the rhetoric, even though we need not make much of the close patterning of language, e.g., Rab's and Yohanan's, where it occurs. The voice of "the Yerushalmi," moreover, authoritatively defines the mode of analysis. The inquiry is consistent and predictable; one argument differs from another not in supposition but only in detail. When individuals' positions occur, it is because what they have to say serves the purposes of the Yerushalmi and its uniform inquiry. The inquiry is into the logic and the rational potentialities of a passage. To these dimensions of thought, the details of place, time, and even of an individual's philosophy, are secondary. All details are turned toward a common core of discourse. This, I maintain, is possible only because the document as a whole takes shape in accord with an overriding program of inquiry and comes to expression in conformity with a single plan of rhetorical expression. To state the proposition simply: it did not just grow by itself, but rather, someone made it up.

The Yerushalmi argument is not indifferent to the chronology of authorities. But the sequence in which things may be supposed to have been said—an early third-century figure's saying before a later fourth-century figure's saying—in no way explains the construction of protracted dialectical arguments. The argument as a whole, its direction and purpose, always govern the selection, formation, and ordering of the parts of the argument and their relationships to one another. The dialectic is determinative. Chronology, if never violated, is always subordinated. Once that fact is clear, it will become further apparent that "arguments"—analytical units of discourse—took shape at the end, with the whole in mind, as part of a plan and a program. That is to say, the components of the argument, even when associated with the names of specific authorities who lived at different times, were not added piece by piece, in order of historical appearance. They were put together whole and complete, all at one time, when the dialectical discourse was made up. By examining a few units of discourse, we shall clearly see the unimportance of the sequence in which people lived, hence of the order in which sayings (presumably) became available.

The upshot is that chronological sequence, while not likely to be ignored, never determines the layout of a unit of discourse. We can never definitively settle the issue of whether a unit of discourse came into being through a long process of accumulation and agglutination, or was shaped at one point—at the end of the time in which named authorities flourished—with everything in hand and a particular purpose in mind. But the more likely of the two possibilities is clearly the latter.

We turn for an illustrative passage to Y. Baba Qamma 2:13. In this protracted discussion, we see how one authority cites another, earlier figure, with the result that the question of consistency of the view of the first authority comes under discussion. Simeon b. Laqish's interpretation of the Mishnah-passage is compared with a view of Hoshaiah, composed earlier by a generation. A further discussion has Ami, slightly later than Simeon b. Laqish, interpret Simeon's view. Then an opinion of Hoshaiah—hence prior to both Ami and Simeon b. Laqish—comes under discussion. The reason is not that Hoshaiah is represented as conducting a face-to-face argument with Simeon or Ami. Hoshaiah's position is formulated quite separately from theirs. But it intersects in topic and logic. Therefore the framer of the whole found it quite natural to cite Hoshaiah's views. The context is the main thing. Ilfai-Hilfa was a contemporary of Yohanan. His position in the construction hardly has been dictated by that fact. Rather, what he has to say forms a final topic of discussion, in sequence after the view of Rab, who surely came earlier in the third century than Ilfai.

The main point bears repeating. We do not find that the chronology of authorities bears any important relationship to the arrangement of opinions. We also do not find violation of the order in which authorities flourished. The long argument has been laid out in accord with the principles of logical exposition at hand. For that purpose no attention needs to be paid to the sequence in which people may have expressed their views. But people of different centuries are not made to talk to one another.

    A. **"How is the tooth deemed an attested danger in regard to eating what is suitable for [eating]" [M. Baba Qamma 1:4C]?**

B. An ox is an attested danger to eat fruit and vegetables.

C. [If, however] it ate [a piece of] clothing or utensils, [the owner] pays half the value of the damage it has caused.

D. Under what circumstances?

E. [When this takes place] in the domain of the injured party.

F. But [if it takes place] in the public domain, he is exempt.

G. But if it [the ox] derived benefit [from damage done in public domain], the owner pays for the value of what [his ox] has enjoyed.

I. A. [To what does the statement, M. 2:3D–G, "Under what circumstances?" apply?] R. Simeon b. Laqish said, "It applies to the first clause. [If, in the public domain, a beast ate what it usually eats, the owner pays nothing. But if, even in the public domain, it ate clothing or utensils, the owner is liable because people commonly leave things in public domain, and the owner of the beast has the responsibility to watch out for such unusual events.]"

B. R. Yohanan said, "It applies to the entire pericope [including the consumption of unusual items, such as clothing or utensils]. [If someone left clothing or utensils in the public domain, the owner of the beast is exempt, because it is not common to leave such things in public domain.]"

C. The opinions imputed to R. Simeon b. Laqish are in conflict.

D. There R. Simeon b. Laqish has said in the name of R. Hoshaiah, "[If] an ox stood still and ate produce which was stacked in piles, [the owner] is liable." [Hence the owner of the beast is liable if the beast eats what it usually eats in the public domain. M. makes no distinction between the beast's doing so while walking along and while standing still.]

E. And here he has said that [the owner is exempt if the beast eats produce in the public domain, on the grounds that that is common.]

F. They said, "There he spoke in the name of R. Hoshaiah while here he speaks in his own name."

II. A. A statement which R. Simeon b. Laqish said: "[If there were two beasts in the public domain, one walking, one crouched and] the one which was walking along butted the one which was crouching, [the owner] is exempt [because the one which was crouching bore responsibility for changing the normal procedure, and it is not normal for a beast to crouch in public domain]."

B. A statement which R. Yohanan said: "[If] the one which was walking along butted the one which was crouching, [the owner] is liable." [The owner of the crouching beast still may ask, "Who gave your beast the right to butt mine?"]

C. [And, Yohanan further will maintain,] it is not the end of the matter that if the one which was walking along butts the one which was crouching, or the one which was crouching butts the one which was walking along, [the owner of the aggressor is liable].

D. But even if the two of them were walking along, and one of those which was walking along butted the other which was walking along, [the owner] is liable [on the same grounds, namely, while both beasts had every right to be where they were, there is no right for one beast to butt the other].

E. [Dealing with these same matters in behalf of Simeon b. Laqish,] R. Ami said, "R. Simeon b. Laqish's position applies only to a case in which a beast which was walking along butted a beast which was crouching, in which case [the owner] is exempt.

F. "But if a beast which was crouching butted one which was walking along, or one which was walking along butted another which was walking along, [the owner in either case] will be liable."

G. R. Hoshaiah taught, "In all cases, [the owner] is exempt."

H. The basis for R. Hoshaiah's position is that liability for injury done by an ox's horn does not apply in public domain anyhow. [Pené Moshe prefers to read:

"This is not a case of damages done by an ox's horn in the public domain."]

I. Rab said, "If the beast stood still [in public domain] and ate up produce which was lying in piles—

J. "now they have made a lenient rule in the case of tooth, in which case an ox walking along consumed produce lying in piles [and so] standing [still],

K. "while they have made a more stringent rule in the case of damages done by the horn,

L. "in which a beast which was walking along has butted a beast which was standing still. [That is, the beast which was walking along does not impose liability on its owner for produce eaten by the way. In this regard a more stringent rule applies to damages done by the beast's horn than those done by the beast's tooth, since if the beast walking along butted one lying down, the owner is liable, while, as we saw, in the case of tooth, the owner is exempt. If, to be sure, the beast had stood still and eaten produce, also in the case of damages done by tooth, the owner is liable.]"

N. Ilfai remarked, "If the beast had stood still and eaten the produce which was lying in piles, [the owner] would be liable.

O. "Now they have made a lenient rule in the case of tooth, in that if the beast which was walking along and ate produce which was lying around, the owner is exempt from paying damages.

P. "But a more stringent rule applies in the case of damages done by the horn when a beast which was walking along butted another beast which was walking along, [and the owner in this case would be liable for damages]."

At Y. Niddah 1:5 we have a mixture of authorities of the same age, the third century, but in different countries. Samuel, in Babylonia, Rab and Yohanan, in the Land of Israel, dispute about the same thing and take diametrically opposed positions. Then Zeira, later on in the same period, comments on what has gone before. Once more the chronology and the logic of what is said are harmonious with one another. But the layout of the discussion as a whole accords with logical principles and how they are to be expounded. The issue of chronology of authorities is not definitive. What comes first are the contrary possibilities of the case. What follows will be the harmonization and contrast of these views. The names are adduced as signs for authorities behind principles, not as indications about the sequence in which things were actually said. That is, the introduction of the second-century figures, Meir and Yose, serves the purpose of linking together their positions on one matter with positions on another matter, held by Samuel and his opposition, a hundred years later. In all, the entire construction seems to be the work of the people who, at the end, gathered together the various opinions or positions and made of them a single continuous argument. That again is the main point.

> A. In what case did they lay down the ruling, "Sufficient for her is her time [of first discovering the drop of menstrual blood, so that there is no prior contamination]"?
>
> B. In the case of [a virgin's, a pregnant woman's, a nursing mother's, or an old woman's] first producing a drop of blood [after missing the period in the latter three instances].
>
> C. But in the instance of the second [or later] producing of a drop of blood, [the blood] imparts uncleanness for the antecedent period of twenty-four hours [by reason of doubt as to when it first occurred].
>
> D. But if [the woman] produced the first drop of blood by reason of constraint [that is, through an abnormal cause], then even in the case of the second drop of blood [we invoke the rule of] sufficiency of the time [of finding the blood for demarcating the commencement of the woman's contaminating power].

> I. A. Samuel said, "This teaching [of A] applies only to a virgin and an old woman. But as to a pregnant woman and a nursing mother, they assign to her the entire period of her pregnancy or the entire period of her nursing [respectively, for the blood ceases, and what does flow is inconsequential, so there is no retroactive contamination at all]."
>
> B. Rab and R. Yohanan—both of them say, "All the same are the virgin, the old woman, the pregnant woman, and the nursing mother [of B]."

C. Said R. Zeira, "The opinion of Rab and R. Yohanan accords with the position of R. Haninah, and all of them differ from the position of Samuel."

D. For R. Eleazar said in the name of R. Haninah, "On one occasion Rabbi gave instruction in accord with the lenient rulings of R. Meir and in accord with the lenient rulings of R. Yose."

E. What was the nature of the case?

F. [If] the fetus was noticeable, and then [the woman] produced a drop of blood—

G. R. Meir says, "She is subject to the rule of the sufficiency of her time [of actually discovering the blood]."

H. R. Yose says, "She imparts uncleanness retroactively for twenty-four hours."

I. [If] she produced many drops of blood, then missed three periods, and afterward produced a drop of blood,

J. R. Meir says, "She imparts uncleanness retroactively for twenty-four hours."

K. R. Yose says, "She is subject to the rule of the sufficiency of her time [of actually discovering blood]."

L. Now if you say that they assign to her the entire period of her pregnancy or the entire period of her nursing, what need do I have for the lenient ruling of R. Yose? The teaching of R. Meir [in such case] produces a still more lenient ruling than does that of R. Yose. [For so far as Meir is concerned, if we read his view in the light of Samuel's opinion (A), the nursing mother and the pregnant woman enjoy the stated leniency throughout the period of nursing or pregnancy. The issue, then, is that Meir deems this drop of blood (I) as a second one. Yose regards the cessation of the period as consequential.]

M. Said R. Mana before R. Yose, "Or perhaps we should assign [Rabbi's ruling] to the case of the milk [dealt with above, in which Meir and Yose dispute about whether the woman who hands over her son to a wet nurse retains the stated leniency. At issue then is whether the matter depends upon the status of the woman's milk or on the status of the child]."

N. He said to him, "The matter was explicitly stated in regard to the present issue. . . ."

The upshot is that we may speak about the Yerushalmi, *its* (authorship's) voice, *its* purposes, *its* mode of constructing a view of the Israelite world. The reason is that, when we claim "the Yerushalmi" speaks, we replicate both the main lines of chronology and the literary character of the document. These point toward the formation of the bulk of materials—its units of discourse—in a process lasting (to take a guess) about half a century, prior to the ultimate arrangement of these units of discourse around passages of the Mishnah and the closure and redaction of the whole into the document we now know.

Let me recapitulate the argument that has led to the conclusion just now stated. The reason, I claim, that we may rely upon the Yerushalmi to testify to the viewpoint of its framers (we assume, a group of sages) at the end point in the Yerushalmi's formation is simple. We rely upon the document as a whole because it speaks, overall, in a uniform voice. It is not merely an encyclopedia of information, but, in general, a sustained, remarkably protracted, uniform inquiry into the logical traits of passages of the Mishnah. Most of the Yerushalmi deals with the exegesis and amplification of the Mishnah's rules. Wherever we turn, that labor of exegesis and amplification, without differentiation in topics or tractates, conforms to a few simple rules in inquiry, repeatedly phrased, implicitly or explicitly, in a few simple rhetorical forms or patterns. These taxonomies repeatedly demonstrate the uniform character of the document as a whole. They furthermore define the essentially simple rules defining that overall character.

Now it is true that the arguments that constitute the exegetical and amplificatory work of the Yerushalmi often contain names of specific authorities. These figures are assumed to have lived not only at the end of the process of the formation of the document, but at the beginning and middle as well. If we could demonstrate that these authorities really said what was attributed to them, we should be able to compose a history of the exegetical process, not merely an account of its end product. We should further hope to relate what people were saying about laws of the Mishnah to the setting in which they did their work. The setting would be susceptible to description in both its social and intellectual dimensions: several periods of history of the Jews of the Land of Israel from 200 to 400 C.E., several sequences of intellectual history (modes of thought, manner of framing questions, ongoing issues, and one-time inquiries). Two hundred years is a long time; much could have happened. Relating the text to its context, not merely over two centuries viewed in retrospect, but decade by decade, will only serve to enlighten us and deepen our understanding of the end product. But, alas, until the end—350-400 C.E.—it turns out that we cannot relate text to context.

We have very good reason to suppose that the text as we have it does speak about the limited context of the period of the actual framing of its principal building blocks. The bulk of this chapter has been devoted to the argument and illustration of that proposition. As I said before, the argument is simple. 1. The building blocks—units of discourse—give evidence of having been put together in a moment of deliberation, in accordance with a plan of exposition, and in response to a finite problem of logical analysis. 2. To state matters negatively, the units of discourse in no way appear to have taken shape slowly, over a long period of time, in a process governed by the order in which sayings were framed, now and here, then and there, later and anywhere else (so to speak). Before us is the result of considered redaction, not protracted accretion, mindful construction, not sedimentary accretion. Now having stated the thesis, I can think of no proof for it, other than the character of the texts themselves. This is why I present numerous examples of the same fundamental aesthetic trait: careful, purposeful redaction, considered formulation. And, as I said at the outset, the traits of the bulk of the Yerushalmi of the Land of Israel may be explained in one of only two ways.

One way is this: the very immediate heirs of the Mishnah, in the opening generation, c. 200-225 C.E., agreed upon conventions not merely of speech and rhetorical formulation, but also of thought and modes of analysis. They further imposed these conventions on all subsequent generations, wherever they lived, whenever they did their work. Accordingly, at the outset the decision was made to do the work precisely in the way in which, two hundred years later, the work turns out to have been done. The alternative view is that, some time late in the formation of diverse materials in response to the Mishnah (and to various other considerations), some people got together and decided to rework whatever was in hand into a single, stunningly cogent document, the Yerushalmi as we know it. Whether this work took a day or a half-century, it was the work of sages who knew precisely what they wished to do, and who did so repeatedly.

This second view is the one I take, and on the basis of it the remainder of this book unfolds. The consequence is that the Yerushalmi exhibits a viewpoint. It is portrayed in what I have called "the Yerushalmi's one voice." So in all, we know what the Yerushalmi's last authorities want us to know. That seems to me a very ample gift of knowledge—not merely of facts—and a generous challenge to our capacities of description, analysis, and interpretation. In the next three chapters we shall examine what the sages propose to say.

2

The Yerushalmi's Picture
of the Sage

While the Yerushalmi aims principally at the exegesis and amplification of the laws of the Mishnah, it also points toward a matrix beyond its text. The Yerushalmi's discussions, to begin with, are not limited to the contents of the Mishnah. Discourse encompasses a world of institutions, authorities, and effective power, quite beyond the imagination of the Mishnah's framers. The Yerushalmi's picture of that world, furthermore, essentially ignores the specifications, for these same matters, of the Mishnah's law. To take one striking example, the Mishnah's government for Israel rests on a high priest and a king, with administrative courts ascending upward to the authority of the Temple mount. The Yerushalmi does not even pretend that such a world exists, knowing in its place a set of small-claims courts and petty bureaus of state, over which sages, defined as judges, lawyers, and masters of disciples in the law, preside. At the head of it all is a patriarch, not a priest anointed for the purpose. This example provides an instance of the curious discontinuity between the Mishnah's view of the world and of the society of Israel, on the one hand, and that of the Yerushalmi, continuous with the Mishnah and framed as little more than an exegesis of that code, on the other hand. The Yerushalmi's picture of the sage as principal authority of the people, Israel, in the Land of Israel, forms the center of that view.

Sages (called by the title of honor, rabbi) are portrayed by the Yerushalmi as exercising authority over not only their own circles, people who agreed with them, but over the Jewish community at large. This authority was practical and involved very specific powers. The first

39

and most important sort of power a sage could exercise under certain circumstances was to sort out and adjudicate rights to property and personal status affecting property. He is described as able to take chattels or real estate from one party and give them into the rightful ownership of some other. The second type of power sages are supposed to have wielded was to tell people what to do, or not to do, in matters not involving property rights. The Yerushalmi alleges that sages could tell people outside the circles of their own disciples and estate how to conduct themselves. A sage is presented as able to coerce someone to do what he might not wish to do, or prevent him from doing what he wants. The first kind of authority may be called judicial, the second, moral. But the distinction is ours, not theirs. The Yerushalmi does not distinguish among the various kinds of authority and power of coercion exercised by sages. Let us now spell out the character of rabbinical authority.

The Yerushalmi takes for granted that sages could define the status of persons in such ways as to affect property and marital rights and standing. It is difficult to imagine a more effective form of social authority. As we shall see, the Yerushalmi treats as settled fact a range of precedents, out of which the character of the law is defined. In those precedents, sages could declare a woman married or free to marry; permit a wife of a priest to eat food in the status of heave offering or prohibit her from doing so; entitle a woman to enjoy the support of a husband's estate or be left without that support; give the right to collect a previously contracted marriage settlement or withhold that right. In all of these ways, as much as in their control of real estate, commerce, and other material and property transactions among Jews, the sages governed the Jewish community as effective political authorities. Whatever beliefs or values they proposed to instill in the people, or realize in the collective life of the community, they effected not through moral suasion or pretense of magic but through sheer political power sanctioned by the government. They could tell people what to do and force them to do it. This is the type of social authority implicit in the Yerushalmi; this is the system of politics attested and assumed in our documents.

The Yerushalmi is remarkably reticent about the basis for rabbis' power over the Jews' political institutions: who bestowed worldly legitimacy to them and supplied the force? To be sure, the systematic provision of biblical proof-texts for Mishnaic laws presents an ample myth for the law. Given by God to Moses at Mount Sinai, the law, including the Mishnah's laws, represents the will of Heaven. But with all the faith in the world, on the basis of such an assertion about God's will, the losing party to a litigation over a piece of real estate will surely have surrendered his property to the other side only with the gravest reservations—if at all. He more likely will have complained to some other authority, if he could. Short of direct divine coercion, upon which a legal system cannot be expected to rely, there had to be more reliable means of making the system work. What these means were, however, the Yerushalmi hardly tells us. So, for the present purpose, we cannot pretend to know. We only know that sages believed that they could run courts and make decisions for Jews who were not sages or disciples.

One thing is clear. Jews did not live in territorial units, ethnically uniform and distinct from areas inhabited by other, equally distinct groups. Every page of the Yerushalmi bespeaks a polyglot and multiform society. Even towns such as Sepphoris and Tiberias, with mainly Jewish populations, are described as sheltering non-Jewish populations, each one with its particular status and rights. What must follow is that the rabbinical courts ruled an ethnic, not a territorial, domain. Cases involving Jews alone would have come to these courts, with other courts doing an equivalent labor for other groups, and provision made (the Yerushalmi hardly hints at its character) for litigation and determination of other juridical questions between members of different ethnic or political units. The rabbis' courts formed only one detail within a political system encompassing a great world beyond, and supporting the small world within, the frame of rabbinical authority.

But of that larger structure of politics and government the Yerushalmi tells us virtually nothing. We have therefore to conclude that the Yerushalmi's perspective is that of a very low level of bureaucracy. In the larger political system, the rabbis' courts constituted a trivial detail. The courts in their hands, powerful though they were in affecting the lives of ordinary Israelites, took up minor matters, with which the great powers of government and state—out there, way up and beyond—did not care to deal. So before us is the world of power portrayed by ethnarchic clerks, nobodies in the larger scheme of things.

It is striking that our document maintains a puzzling silence regarding not only the relationship of the rabbinical courts to the larger political structure upon which the actions of those courts had to depend, but also as striking is the relationship of the sages as judges and administrators to other Jewish community judges and administrators who may have carried out the same tasks and exercised the same responsibilities in regard to the Jewish nation of the Land of Israel. While, to be sure, unlike the case of the Babylonian Talmud's account of matters, we hear no complaints about unqualified judges—people executing decisions not based upon sound knowledge of the law, hence, nonrabbinic

Jewish judges at work in the Jewish nation—we hardly may take for granted that the Yerushalmi tells us all of the facts about the Jewish political structure of the Land of Israel. So on what basis was the Mishnah adopted as the sole legitimate law of the Jewish nation in its Land (if indeed all law derived from the Mishnah)? And at what time did the Jewish political agencies (the court, administration, school), established by the imperial government to take charge of the Jewish nation, hand over authority to a bureaucracy of clerks made up solely of people trained in the Mishnah? These are pressing questions to which we have no answers at all.

So we come to a puzzling fact. The Yerushalmi describes as natural and normal a world in which the Mishnah is the sole law of Israel, and sages are the only qualified authorities to govern Israel in accord with the law of the Mishnah. But the Yerushalmi nowhere celebrates the victory of its authorities and the law it presents over competing authorities and law. It hardly suggests competition of any sort between sages and others bearing competing qualifications, or exercising authority to govern without rabbinical approval and appointment. Even if we concede that the Yerushalmi's picture accurately portrays the state of affairs of the Yerushalmi's own time—the last half of the fourth century—we still do not know when questions of the authority of the Mishnah's law and the power of the Mishnah's masters were settled in just this way. Was it in c. 200 C.E., when the Mishnah was closed and "published"? What system of law, then, did the Mishnah replace, and why did the people who enforced that other system give way? These two questions, like the two in the foregoing paragraph, merely suggest the range of inquiry presently closed to all imaginable initiative. They only adumbrate the dimensions of the realm of sovereign darkness: the political context in which the Yerushalmi speaks and of which we are totally uninformed.

We turn to what we do know, namely, the Yerushalmi's picture of what the sages (clerks of the Jewish ethnic government in Palestine, for example, the nasi, or patriarch, of Israel in the Land of Israel) could force people to do because of their political power and position. To be emphasized at the outset is the distance from their world to ours. We are used to regarding some questions as secular, others as religious, some as political, others as moral. We realize sages perceived no such distinction. We take for granted that the sage as a supernatural figure is to be described in one setting, the sage as politician in a second, the sage as a judge in a third, the sage as a religious teacher in a fourth, the sage as a teacher in a fifth, and so on. So we envision the holy man in a cave, politician in the court of the Jewish patriarch, judge in his court in the piazza, preacher in the synagogue pulpit (to continue the stupefying anachronism!), the teacher in the schoolroom. But the sage in his time, as his document describes it, was always and everywhere all of these things at once: the same names appear in every role with slight differentiation. Specialization in the arts of the supernatural or the political was unthinkable. So the same sage who was believed able to make rain or stop a pestilence also decided how a contract had to be carried out, who was free to marry whom, and which party to a litigation owned a particular plot in a vegetable garden. It is one thing to acknowledge that political figures also have charismatic charm. It is quite another to come to grips with the detailed facts of the integration, in the person of the sage, of this world with the world above, the world to come, and all other worlds, principalities, and powers anyone in that age could imagine or conjure.

The Yerushalmi does not allow us to recognize this, giving us only lawyer-magicians, philosopher-politicians. We meet teachers worried about controlling the weather and administering healing to the sick, while also telling Mrs. Cohen she may eat her husband's holy rations for breakfast, and Mr. Levi to support his stepmother, Mr. Isaac to hand over his back lot to his neighbor, the rightful owner, and Mr. Jacob to fulfill his contract. The same names appear in every context in which the exercise of authority is at issue. But to make sense of that authority, as I said, we have to sort out its types, attempt to classify each story in which one party told another party what to do and made his instructions stick. That is the purpose of the next four sections, with their rapid survey of types of rabbinical authority as portrayed by the Yerushalmi.

The single most striking trait of reports about what sages said and did as judges in courts is the practical character of the authority imputed to sages. From the perspective of the late fourth century, as I said, sages are viewed as judges able to take property from one party and assign it to some other. That picture is drawn simply, always en passant. Litigants are portrayed not solely as disciples of sages but also as ordinary folk. Decisions are carried out not by persuasion or threats of supernatural retaliation but through coercion (though the political basis is not specified). Appealing to a different court, for example, one instituted by the imperial government, never appears as an avenue explored by the losing party. More important, and surely probative, rabbis' complaints against Jews' appeals to gentile courts do not occur, to my knowledge. It follows that, in their view, rabbinical judges exercised unchallenged de jure power in their courts. Here I think we have to believe the rabbis' picture. Jewish authorities enjoyed certain limited power over the conduct of everyday life, including all manner of material transactions. Upon that simple fact the tales before us stand in agreement. As testimonies to the ongoing state of affairs, they provide solid evidence on how judges themselves saw things at the time the stories came to closure and redaction.

We begin our brief survey of the Yerushalmi's picture of the sage as judge with the most striking kind of power, that exercised over title to land. Possession of real estate conferred the status of householder. It represented ownership of true capital, however insubstantial. The power to transfer ownership from one party to another, or to govern transactions with that same effect, thus represents the single most important testimony to the character of the authority of the sage as judge. Courts exercising authority over an ethnic group spread out among other ethnic groups need not have enjoyed jurisdiction over real estate transactions. Indeed, unless both parties to a dispute were Jews, I do not see how the Jewish national or ethnic courts of the Land could have exercised jurisdiction. But the Yerushalmi's authorities believed their courts could settle litigation over the title to land and the sale of land by minors. These reports, the first on a defense against a claim of title by usucapion, the second on the sale of real property by a minor, leave no doubt as to the Yerushalmi's view of the state of affairs.

Y. Baba Batra 3:3.III

A. R. Yose b. Haninah asked R. Yohanan, "[If the owner of a property] enters a complaint [against the squatter], what is the law as to his having to do so before a court?"

B. R. Yose in the name of R. Yohanan: "[If] one raises a complaint, he does not have to do so before a court."

C. There are those who teach [the aforestated matter as follows:]

D. R. Yose b. R. Haninah asked the disciples of R. Yohanan, "[If the owner of a property] raises a complaint [against the squatter], what is the law as to his having to do so before a court?"

E. R. Hiyya in the name of R. Yohanan: "[If] one raises a complaint, he must do so before a court."

F. Samuel said, "Even if one has raised a complaint with [the squatter] before the workers, that constitutes a valid act of complaint."

G. And does one have to enter a complaint for each of the

three years [at the outset, or, if the property is held over a long period of years, must the complaint be entered annually even after the first three years' complaints]?

H. Gidul bar Minyamin had a case [in which he had entered a complaint for the first three years only]. The judges of his case were Hilqiah bar Tobi, R. Huna, and Hiyya bar Rab. Hiyya bar Rab said to them, "Thus did father say: 'Once he has entered a complaint against [the squatter] for the first three years, he does not again have to enter a complaint against him.'"

Y. Baba Batra 9:6.III

D. A youth sold his property, and the case came before R. Hiyya bar Joseph and R. Yohanan, [since the relatives claimed that he sold the property as a minor and had no power to do so].

E. R. Hiyya bar Joseph ruled, "The prevailing supposition is that [the witnesses signed the deed] for a person of mature mind [and the purchaser of the property has the advantage]."

F. R. Yohanan ruled, "Since [the purchaser] has come to remove property from the family, it is his burden to bring proof [that the youth was of mature capacities when he made the sale of his property]."

The importance of the preceding case reports lies in their offhand tone. In both instances it is taken for granted that sages judge cases involving real estate, drawing upon their own legal traditions to settle the issues. We notice no sign that we have court documents in hand, since there is no recurrent formal pattern so indicating. These are reports in the setting of the analysis of legal theory, as indicated by the inquiry to disciples (Yose to Yohanan's). The theoretical character of the reports is shown, further, in the preservation of two distinct opinions at Y. Baba Batra 9:6. There are two possible grounds for settling the case, and each is specified. Accordingly, the Yerushalmi's reports are true to its character as a set of notes on discourse about law. But embedded within these reports is the prevailing assumption that actual cases have come to hand.

As I said, if sages as judges maintained they could transfer ownership of the prized form of capital, land, we cannot be surprised that they claimed jurisdiction over lesser chattels and transactions in movables. Such issues involving conflicting claims on the terms of a property lease, and appropriate utilization of property subject to neighbors' rights, are portrayed in the next examples. In the former instance, the rabbinical judge is represented as making a decision in light of what was perceived as sound social policy—keeping land ownership out of the hands of Gentiles (here, an Aramaean)—and not merely in accordance with the strict requirements of the law. But Jews alone are involved. In other cases, the comfort and convenience of parties to a common courtyard had to be sorted out, again a typically domestic issue.

Y. Baba Mesia 8:9.II

> A. Now he who rented a house to his fellow and then proposed to sell it [during the rental period, to a third party] —
>
> B. Said R. Ami, "It was not with the stipulation that the owner should die from hunger [that the agreement was made]." [If the owner needs to sell the house in order to support himself and his family, he has that right.]
>
> C. Both R. Zira and R. Hela say, "Under all circumstances it is deemed acquired by the new purchaser.
>
> D. "But the landlord [who has sold the house] says [to the purchaser], 'Let him be, for it is available to the tenant until his lease runs out.'"
>
> E. A case came before R. Nisi, who did not accept [the position of Zira and Hela].
>
> F. Why did he differ from them?
>
> G. They say, The house in question was assigned as a pledge to a certain Roman [Aramaean]. [If the landlord could not sell it right away and so redeem it from the Gentile, the house would have fallen into the Gentile's ownership.] It was on that account that he ruled in accordance with R. Ami [that the sale must be consummated forthwith].

Y. Baba Batra 2:3.III

> E. R. Abimi bar Tobi gave instructions to put a dung heap [or: loom] between one wall and another wall.

F. R. Isaac bar Haqilah gave instruction to a lumber mill to set [the sawing] at a distance of four cubits from the wall of his property.

Y. Baba Batra 2:3.I

A. R. Jacob bar Aha drove a pastry seller from one portico to another [that is, forced him to move away].

B. There was a pastry seller [who] opened [a store] under [the dwelling of] R. Abedomi, brother of R. Yose. R. Aha passed by and did not object [to the opening of the store]. [R. Abedomi] said, "Rabbis pass by and do not object [to this store]!" R. Aha grew angry with him. R. Abedomi, brother of R. Yose, grew sick. He became yet sicker. R. Yose came up to call on him. He said, "I shall go and raise the question with [Aha]." He went and spoke, and the court [on which Aha sat] gave instructions to have pity on him and to prepare burial shrouds for him [as a sign that Aha had made his peace with the brother].

C. A man sold off his entire courtyard, leaving for himself one porch only. He would go up and sit there. The case came before R. Jonah b. R. Yose. They ruled, "You have no right to go up and sit on the porch and watch [the owner] go in and come out of his house."

D. A man sold off half of his courtyard. He left for himself one bread shop [already situated in the courtyard]. The case came before R. Jonah and R. Yose. They ruled, "You are the one who came to him. He never came to you."

E. And so it was taught:

F. If the stall or the shop was there before the granary, [the owner of the granary] does not have the power to object.

In the first of the three cases, considerations of national policy took precedence over the established law. In the matter of the Aramaean, retrieving the house and placing it into Israelite ownership was the prime consideration. Accordingly, the vision of the rabbinical clerk took in a broader landscape than the law alone. In the second, sages ruled on the rights of neighbors to be protected from nuisances. In the third, there is a curious mixture of law and supernatural intervention. The sage who was the injured party complained of the failure of the rabbinical authority to protect his rights. The latter then grew angry, and the former fell ill and died. It goes without saying that if the displeasure of the clerk was believed to bring such serious consequences, ordinary folk who believed such was the case would be careful to avoid angering a sage. But in context the authority of the bureaucrat is not represented as resting upon the state of his emotions. We do not know just what sanctions came into play, but we have no reason at this point to believe the disposition of real estate and rights to the disposition of property depended solely on the feelings of the sage.

The sale and disposition of real estate did not normally take place in the context of active speculation in land. Rather, land and houses were transferred as part of gifts, generally as gifts of contemplation of death or with the transfer of a woman and her dowry, that is, her share in her father's estate, from father to husband and, in the event of divorce, back to her father's house. Instances involving gifts of property, including real estate, in contemplation of death, include the following cases decided by rabbinical judges.

Y. Qiddushin 1:5.III

> O. When a certain man was dying, he said, "Let all my property be given to Mr. So-and-so." Then he went and said, "Let it be written over in a deed and given to him." [He then died.]
>
> P. [The problem is whether it was the donor's intention to give the property over only through a deed. But such a deed is invalid if issued after the testator's death. So] R. Eleazar and R. Simeon b. Yaqim brought the case to R. Yohanan.
>
> Q. He ruled, "If he made that statement in order to transfer ownership to him, all concur that the donee has acquired ownership. If he made that statement in order to give him ownership through a deed, all concur that a man does not impart ownership through a deed after death. [What a dying man says is deemed done. Hence if the statement was merely to strengthen the donee's claim on the property, it was valid as soon as it was made. But if the statement was to do the whole transfer by deed, then as soon as the man died, the

instructions he gave on drawing up the deed are null.]"

Y. Ketubot 11:1.VII

A. R. Yudan fled to Noy [where Yose was domiciled]. A case came before R. Yose: "A dying man who said, 'Let the bonds of So-and-so [my bonds] be handed over to So-and-so' [what is the law? Has this statement transferred ownership of the bonds?]"

B. He said to him, "A dying man transfers ownership by a mere verbal declaration only of things which are transferred by a healthy person either through a deed or through an act of drawing the object to the recipient.

C. "But these are acquired through drawing or through a deed . . ."

D. "A boat is acquired through drawing."

E. "R. Nathan says, 'A boat and documents are acquired through drawing and through a writ' [Y. Qiddushin 1:7A–B].

F. "If one wrote a deed but did not draw the object, or drew the object but did not write a deed, he has accomplished nothing—unless he both writes a deed and draws the object."

What is important in the foregoing is that the rabbinical courts clearly took for granted the power to govern the transfer of title to land. The point at issue, the technicalities of the transfer of title in a case of a gift in contemplation of death, was secondary.

We come to yet another sort of gift, namely, a gift of real estate by a father to a son so that he might marry and start his own family. The issue here is whether movables passed with the real estate.

Y. Ketubot 5:1.III

E. This statement accords with that which R. Hanania said: "He who marries off his son in a house—the son has acquired ownership of the house. And that rule is on condition that it is the first marriage of the son."

F. R. Hoshaiah taught, "He has acquired ownership of

the movables, but he has not acquired ownership of the house itself."

G. How does he differ [from Hanania]?

H. R. Jeremiah in the name of R. Abbahu: "Interpret [Hoshaiah's] statement to speak of a case in which the father's granary was in the house. [Accordingly, the father uses the house and does not intend to give it away.]"

I. R. Hezekiah in the name of R. Joshua b. Levi, "[That point is self-evident.] It was necessary [to indicate that] even if there were things in the house which had been borrowed from the marketplace, [the son has not acquired ownership of the house]. [Even if used for such a purpose as temporary storage, the house remains in the domain of the father.]"

J. Said R. Abbahu, "If [the father had made it explicit to the son that he was merely] lending him the house for the purpose of the marriage, then the son has not acquired ownership even [of the movables which are in the house]."

K. A case of this sort came before R. Jacob b. R. Bun, and he decided it in accordance with the view of R. Abbahu.

Once more we note that the case report is preserved only in the setting of a discussion of legal theory. Whether the purpose of the report is merely to preserve the fact or to indicate the decided law is unclear. For our purposes it is significant as evidence that sages took for granted that they could make practical decisions of this kind.

Finally, a woman might exercise the right to own and sell real estate. At the same time, she possessed only limited rights to support from the husband. Accordingly, the husband enjoyed a lien on her property, since she could not sell her real property and then claim to be impoverished and so require his support. While she held title to her real estate, the property was indentured to the husband. A concrete case follows.

Y. Baba Batra 8:8.II

HH. A woman deeded her property as a gift to a certain person. She fell into need and sold her property to her husband. R Hiyya bar Madayya brought the

case before R. Yose [with the following argument]:
"Did not R. Yannai say, 'Rabbi concurs that the first
may not give over this property under the law of
gifts in contemplation of death'? [That is, the
woman was in the status of the first of the sequence
of recipients. In Rabbi's view, such a person has the
right to ownership of the property itself, and, consequently, just as, if the man should sell the property,
it is a valid sale, so here too, if the woman disposed
of the property, it is valid.]"

II. [Yose] said to [Hiyya], "R. Yohanan [holds] also
that it does not fall into the category of the gift of a
healthy person [so the woman cannot dispose of the
property in any wise, but must keep it and derive
benefit from it throughout her lifetime]. [Conse-
quently, she cannot dispose of it at all through a
donation. Her gift of the property was null.]

JJ. "In the case of the woman, since her husband was
liable to provide her maintenance, her deed does not
fall into the category of the gift in contemplation of
death. [During her lifetime she cannot dispose of
the property, since it is indentured to the husband.
She cannot sell it for her own needs, since the
husband provides for her. Hence any disposition of
the land falls after death, at which point the heirs
take precedence over someone to whom she might
have proposed to give or sell the land. The prior
transaction was null.]"

Here the legal discussion flows from a case report, but the shift in
the character of discourse makes no difference. The right of the rabbinical court to dispose of the issue is taken for granted by the narrator.

Conflicting claims against estates, of course, involved movables and
goods as much as real estate. First, old scores might be settled through
litigation against an heir's claim to a common estate, as in the first story
that follows. Second, since a widow was supported by the estate until she
received full payment of the marriage settlement coming to her upon the
death of her husband, as a primary lien against the husband's estate, the
rights of a widow come into conflict with those of the heirs to the estate.
She would want to be supported for as long as possible, thus to postpone
receiving payment of her marriage settlement. The heirs would want to

be rid of her as soon as possible. Along these same lines, female heirs, seeking a dowry from the estate, and male heirs, seeking division of the estate so that they could gain possession of their property or capital, came into conflict.

Y. Baba Batra 9:3.IV

    C. A man became a scribe [at the expense of the father, who had paid the tuition for his studies]. His brothers wanted to divide [his salary with him]. The case came before R. Ami. He said, "Thus do we rule: 'A person who found an object—do his brothers share it with him?' [Obviously not.]"

    D. A man went out on a mission [for a salary]. His brothers wanted to divide [his salary] with him. The case came before R. Ami. He said, "Thus do we rule: 'A man who went out and made his living as a bandit—do his brothers share [his booty] with him?'"

    E. R. Horaina, brother of R. Samuel bar Suseretai—his brother wanted to divide up [what each party was making, that is, form a common pot of their earnings or profits]. He said to him, "Alexander, my brother, you know that our father left us two thousand. [You yourself know what father left us. There were only two thousand of his. Whatever there is in addition is what I myself earned when father was alive, and it is mine, not part of the estate.]"

Y. Baba Batra 9:1.I

    X. This is in line with the following [which shows that a claim for settlement of the marriage contract ends the right of support]:

    Y. The widow of R. Shobetai was wasting the assets of the estate [by spending too much on her own maintenance]. The children came and approached R. Eleazar. He said to them, "What can we do for you? You are foolish people, [you have no remedy against her]."

    Z. When they went out, they said, "As to her marriage settlement, what should we do?"

AA. Someone told them, "Pretend to sell some of the estate's property, and she will come and lay claim for her marriage settlement, on account of which she will lose the claim of support from the estate."

BB. After some days she came and approached R. Eleazar. He said to her, "May a curse come upon me, if I said a thing to them."

CC. [He said,] "Now what can I do for you, for it is a blow of deceivers [Pharisees] which has struck you."

Y. Ketubot 6:6.II

J. [What is the law as to collecting dowry for daughters from indentured property when there is a fixed value assigned to the dowry? That is, after the father died, the brothers took the property and mortgaged it. May the daughters collect their dowry from this mortgaged property, retrieving it for that purpose from the possession of the purchaser?] Said R. Zeira, "R. Yohanan would not permit collection [under such circumstances]."

K. Who orders collection [of the dowry from the mortgaged property]? R. Haninah [and R. Ilai] do so.

L. R. Yosa was trustee for the estate of orphans, and some of the daughters sought support [for their weddings]. The case came before R. Eleazar and R. Simeon b. Yaqim. Ruled R. Simeon b. Yaqim, "Is it not better that they should be supported from the property of their father, and not from public charity?"

M. Said to him R. Eleazar, "If such a matter should come before our sages, though, they would not touch it. Shall we then decide a practical case in this way? [That is, they are not sure of the law.]"

N. Said to R. Yose, "I shall provide for them, and if the [male] orphans should come and complain, I shall provide for them too [by retrieving from the girls and giving to the boys]."

O. Even so, the heirs knew about the decision and entered no complaint.

P. R. Zeira asked before R. Yose, "How do they decide a practical case?"

Q. He said to him, "In accordance with the view of R. Haninah [K]."

R. So the case came from court, decided in accord with the view of R. Haninah.

S. [Disagreeing with this position, said] R. Abun in the name of R. Hela: "They regard the property as if it were destroyed [and totally unavailable, and they do not collect from it for the present purpose]."

The rulings of Ami, Y. Baba Batra 9:3, show the sage as a judge settling family disputes about property. The item involving Horaina is not presented as a court case, but the issue is the same. Accordingly, to the framer of the passage the difference between a case settled by a rabbinical clerk, presumably for outsiders to the rabbinical estate, and one in which sages simply gave their opinions, is null. All stories and cases serve the same purpose, which is to expose the potentialities of the law. But the stories about court settlements and decisions indicate a clear-cut statement that sages decided such matters as these. In the second item, Y. Baba Batra 9:1, Eleazar informs the plaintiffs that his court can do nothing for them, because the law is against them. The people found their own remedy. But the clerk's incapacity stemmed from the substance of the law, not the weakness of his court's authority. The final case shows us a similar situation, in which legal theory and practice were treated on a single plane.

While authority over real transactions in real estate, gifts, and testaments is most striking, ordinary folk would more regularly have encountered rabbinical authority in litigating conflicts of movables, especially arising in trade and commerce, as well as in collection of debts and bailments. These kinds of cases, being trivial in value as compared to those entailing transfer of real property, are apt to have been more common. Breach of contract, for example in commercial transactions, came under rabbinical supervision.

Y. Baba Mesia 4:2.II

D. R. Hiyya bar Joseph handed over a denar to a salt merchant for salt. The latter party retracted [as salt went up in price]. He said to him, "Do you not know that a scythe will cut into your thigh: He who extracted punishment from the men of the Generation of the Flood is destined to exact punishment from him who does not keep his word [M. Baba Mesia 4:2F]."

E. A man handed over money for silk. [The seller] retracted. The case came before R. Hiyya bar Joseph and R. Yohanan. R. Hiyya bar Joseph said, "Either give him [silk] of the value of what he has left as a pledge [in advance of the purchase, which was not the entire purchase price], or submit to the curse, 'He who exacted punishment . . .'"

F. R. Yohanan ruled, "Either give him all which he has purchased, or accept the curse, 'He who exacted punishment . . .'"

The sanction for breach of contract is a curse, as specified. The power of the sage to call down that curse clearly is taken for granted, and the curse is treated as a perfectly routine court procedure. In this instance, therefore, the rabbi's authority depended upon his imputed status as a supernatural figure; this contrasts with the cases in which the clerk's adjudication of a real estate matter in no way involved magical sanctions.

One form of contract sages would not enforce involved usury, defined as "payment for waiting for one's money." The bulk of the stories in hand, however, narrate transactions involving sages themselves, so we cannot show that ordinary folk could or did bring suit in this regard.

Y. Baba Mesia 5:6.IV

A. Abba bar Zamina gave a denar to the baker and bought bread from him at the lowest prevailing price throughout the year.

B. Now Rab did not approve this arrangement [seeing it as payment for waiting for repayment of the money].

C. R. Hiyya the Elder had some flax. Ass drivers came to buy it from him. He said to them, "I was not thinking of selling now, but rather at the time at which the crop is more abundant [and demand greater]."

D. They said to him, "Sell it to us now, in accord with the price which you will get if you sell it later when the crop is more abundant."

E. He came and asked Rabbi.

F. He said to him, "It is forbidden, [for this looks as if he is being paid for waiting on repayment of funds]."

The prohibition of usury carried in its wake the view that gold and silver were to be treated as commodities. The issue of fluctuations in the value of gold and silver then brought litigation to court, as did the claim that services had been rendered in exchange for a loan and thus usury had occurred.

Y. Baba Mesia 4:1.I

F. The implication of what Rabbi has said is that gold is in the status of a commodity.

G. We have a Mishnah teaching which states, "Silver is in the status of a commodity."

H. The daughter of R. Hiyya the Elder lent Rab [golden] denars. She came and asked her father [how to collect the debt, since in the meantime, gold had risen in value vis-à-vis silver]. He said to her, "Take from him good and substantial denars [of the same weight as those you lent]."

I. From the daughter of R. Hiyya, shall we learn [that gold is deemed a commodity]? [Perhaps there was some other consideration which led to Hiyya's advising her as he did.]

J. Said R. Idi, "Also Abba, father of Samuel, raised the question before Rabbi: 'What is the law as to lending [golden] denars for the return of [the same weight in golden] denars?' He said to him, 'It is permitted [to do so].'"

K. Said R. Jacob bar Aha, "Also R. Yohanan and R. Simeon b. Laqish both say that it is permitted to lend [golden] denars for the return of the [same weight in golden] denars."

Y. Baba Mesia 5:1.VI

A. He who lends money to his fellow [should not live in his courtyard for free, nor should he pay less than the prevailing rate, for that is tantamount to usury (M. Baba Mesia 5:1)].

    B. A man lent money to his fellow. The latter let him space in his building. Later on the borrower said to the lender, "Pay me the rent for my building."

    C. The lender said to him, "Give me back my money. [I had assumed you would not charge me rent so long as my money was in your hands.]"

    D. The case came before R. Ba bar Mina. He ruled, "Now does [the lender] get what he had imagined was free [merely because he assumed it]? [Obviously not! He was wrong and has no claim at all.]"

The two cases concerning the status of precious metals involve sages and their families. The third one, by contrast, indicates that usury in kind was an issue before the courts, and that common folk brought such cases. Whether the courts would enforce the prohibition against usury under ordinary circumstances is not clear, and we do not know if they had the jurisdiction. Still, I do not know why the clerks would have been denied this, given their reports about their other powers.

Rabbinical courts were called upon to settle cases involving collection of debts. As in the case of breach of contract, their power involved imposition of frightening oaths, which people tried to avoid. The rabbinical judges claimed the power to force the collection of outstanding debts, not only from the debtor himself, but also from the guarantor of the debt. They also imposed their own reading on bonds of indebtedness in a case in which the writing was unclear. Finally, they assumed full authority to determine the facts of the matter.

Y. Shebuot 6:2.IV

    A. R. Merinus served as a pledge for someone who borrowed money from his daughter-in-law. The case [of the daughter-in-law's claim] came before R. Hama, father of Bar Qappara, and R. Hoshaiah. After confessing in court [that he had served as a pledge for the debt and was obligated to pay it,] he said, "But I already paid it."

    B. They asked R. Hiyya the Elder. He went and asked Rabbi. Rabbi replied, "He who by court decision is obligated to pay a debt does not have the power [to claim that he had already paid it]."

Y. Baba Batra 10:1.V

H. A bill of indebtedness went from R. Huna [who made no decision on how to read it] to R. Shimi, on which the word *ogdoe* [of *ogdoeconta*, (eighty)] was erased, and *conta* was clear.

I. Said R. Shimi to R. Huna, "Go and see what is the lowest numeral in Greek that conta is combined with."

J. He said, "It is *triaconta* (thirty)."

K. When the party had left, he said, "That man intended to make thirty [by the erasure] and lost twenty [the original was *penteconta* (fifty)]."

Y. Sanhedrin 3:8.IV

A. R. Abbahu in the name of R. Yohanan: "He who hides his witnesses behind a wall [to entrap another party] has not accomplished anything."

B. It is in line with the following: There was a man who wanted to join a banquet.

C. [The host] said to him, "Will you give me what you owe me?"

D. He said to him, "Yes."

E. After they got up from the banquet, [the unwanted guest] said to him, "I don't owe you anything at all."

F. [The host] said to him, "I have witnesses [that you confessed to the debt]."

G. [The defendant] said to him, "I only said that because I didn't want to ruin your banquet."

H. The case came before R. Ami, who ruled, "This is in line with that which R. Yohanan has stated, 'He who hides his witnesses behind a wall has not accomplished anything.'"

These rather routine reports leave no doubt that sages maintained they could order payment of debts. We have no clear evidence on the actual procedures, particularly with reference to the sort of sanctions sages could impose if their orders were not obeyed. The first of the three cases involved a sage, but the others make clear that ordinary folk, not bound by the disciplines of the rabbinical estate, were under the jurisdiction of the clerks.

The rabbinical courts dealt not only with property, but also with threats to sound social policy. For instance, the sale of animals to Gentiles was discouraged, whether on grounds that the beasts might serve some idolatrous purpose, that the beasts would be so worked as to violate the Sabbath law, or that the raising of small cattle posed a severe threat to the ecology of the land. Accordingly, a penalty quite outside normal judicial procedures was imposed in the following instance.

Y. Abodah Zarah 1:6.IV

> D. [There is this precedent.] A certain person sold a camel to an Aramaean. The case came before R. Simeon b. Laqish, who imposed a penalty on him of twice the proceeds, so that [the Israelite] would go after the [Aramaean purchaser] and recover the camel.
>
> E. Said R. Yose b. R. Bun, "[Simeon b. Laqish] imposed the fine on the middleman, [and not on the Israelite who had sold the beast to the middleman], and they used to insult [the child of the middleman], 'A son of the Aramaeans' agent!'"
>
> F. [In imposing such a fine, even though, in law, the man was exempt from such a fine,] R. Simeon b. Laqish was in accord with R. Judah.

Torts involving cultic, as against merely material, damage naturally came to rabbinical courts, just as is the case today.

Y. Sanhedrin 1:1.VI

> A. A man deliberately rendered a priest [cultically] unclean. The case came before R. Isaac, and he ordered the man to provide unconsecrated food for the priest to eat [since he could not eat cheaper food in the status of heave offering, which he normally ate, by reason of his cultic uncleanliness].

These cases have in common the presence of issues of a nonmaterial character. In the former case, the rabbinical court imposed a heavy fine so as to discourage a deleterious practice. In the latter the violation of the taboo affecting the man brought in its wake an additional cost; this had to be compensated. It is clear that, in their minds, sages bore responsibility for more than ordinary real estate and commercial transactions. They were judicial and social authorities.

The power of the court to summon a litigant or a witness rested upon the capacity to declare a recalcitrant party to be ostracized or excommunicated. This had the effect of removing him from the Jewish community. Since the penalty is taken for granted as effective, we learn that the sages behind the tale assumed general support from the Jewish community for their judicial activities.

Y. Moed Qatan 3:1.VII

> A. R. Joshua b. Levi summoned a man to his court three times, and the man did not come. He sent him the message, "If it were not the case that in my entire life I have never declared a man to be subject to a herem (ostracism), I should have declared you to be in herem."
>
> B. For twenty-four reasons they excommunicated a person, and this is one of them.
>
> C. "And that if any one did not come within three days, by order of the officials and the elders all his property should be forfeited, and he himself banned from the congregation of the exiles" (Ezra 10:8).
>
> D. Said R. Isaac b. R. Eleazar, "There are many more than those twenty-four cases scattered throughout the Mishnah."

For the penalty of ostracism to work, there had to be general compliance with rabbis' authority. Yet the sanction was invoked, in particular, to force compliance with the court's procedures, not obedience to its decisions in a case of conflicting property claims. There a more formidable sanction had to come into play, for the courts could hardly depend for effective authority only upon a common consensus about something that to begin with, was subject to conflict.

If the Jewish nation at large accepted the sovereignty of rabbinical courts in property disputes, the reason may have been the power of the courts not only to persuade or elicit general support, but also to call upon the power of the state to transfer ownership of real and movable property from one party to another. We come now to a kind of jurisdiction which, in the end, had to enjoy not merely passive acquiescence through fear of ostracism but active support of the people at large, namely, determinations of personal status. While the courts might call upon the state to back up their rulings about property, they are not likely to have enjoyed equivalent support in matters to which the government was probably indifferent, such as whether a given woman was betrothed and not free to marry anyone but the fiancé, or whether she was not betrothed and so free to marry anyone of her choice. Persistent meddling in such affairs could have generated only widespread protest, unless the community at large acquiesced and indeed actively supported the right of the courts to make such decisions. Nonetheless, even behind these evidences of rabbinical authority, based as they are on sanctions of moral authority, as distinct from the imperial government's ultimate threat of force, there still were elements of exchange of property or things of value. Consequently, when we deal with personal status, we take up yet another aspect of the rabbi's power to judge property cases. For rulings in cases involving personal status—whether or not a woman was betrothed or married, a slave was freed, a man was a valid priest—always carried in their wake material considerations. Indeed, even if the courts were set up only to settle questions of personal status in accordance with the law of the Jewish nation, something of slight concern to the government, the courts would have had to enjoy the power to transfer real property and movables from one party to another. We may hardly be surprised, therefore, to find a substantial repertoire about how sages decided questions of the status of women, slaves, and similar sorts of persons in a subordinate or otherwise special status.

As we follow the story of a marriage from beginning to end, that is, from betrothal to either divorce or the death of the husband, we sequentially compile reports of how sages intervened in judging important cases down the line. At the outset there was the matter of stipulations made in a writ of betrothal and whether or not these had been met by the specified deadline. The first passage states the law, the second, a case involving application of the law.

Y. Gittin 7:6.II

> A. Said R. Abbahu in the name of R. Yohanan: "The provisions of a conditional writ of betrothal are as follows:
>
> B. "I, So-and-so, son of Such-and-such, betroth you, Miss So-and-so, daughter of Such-and-such, on the stipulation that I give you such-and-such a sum of money,

and that I marry you by such-and-such a date. If that
date comes and I have not married you, I shall have no
claim whatsoever on you.' "

C. What if an untoward event took place [preventing the
marriage, not through the fault of the prospective
groom]? [Is the writ deemed null?]

D. R. Yohanan said, "The accident is as if it did not
happen [and the betrothal is null]. [An accident is no
excuse.]"

E. R. Simeon b. Laqish said, "The accident most certainly
did happen [and we take it into account]. [Since it
was through no fault of the groom that the betrothal
did not lead to a marriage, the writ remains valid and
may be carried out.]"

F. In the view of R. Simeon b. Laqish, the groom had to
carry out the stipulation. If the day came and he did
not marry her, then, [as the writ says,] "I shall have
no claim whatsoever on you."

G. When R. Yohanan was dying, he gave instructions
to his daughters to carry out the law in accordance
with the opinion of R. Simeon b. Laqish, for a court
later on may concur with him, in which case [my]
grandchildren will be in the position of mamzers
[since the court will declare the writ to be valid]. [If
the daughters do not then enter into the stipulated
marriage, but marry another party, they will have
violated a valid writ of betrothal, and, with the women
deemed betrothed to one party, should they produce
children by another, the children will be in the status
of mamzers.]

H. A man paid in advance to a canal barge operator, but
the canal went dry [so the bargeman could not trans-
port the produce to market]. The case came before
R. Nahman bar Jacob. [If the defendant claims,]
"Here is the barge, bring me the canal" [Nahman
accepts the plea].

I. Abba bar Huna in the name of R. Abba [who does not
accept the claim of an untoward accident] held that
the farmer hoped that the canal would dry up, so he
could take his money back.

Y Qiddushin 3:2.III

A. [If,] once the time came [for the marriage,] the pro-spective husband claims, "I have done [what I prom-ised in the writ of betrothal]," while she claims, "I have not received [what he promised],"—

B. R. Abun said, "Since he seeks to retrieve the writ of betrothal from the woman, it is his task to bring proof. [She wishes to stand by the document, that is to say, the condition has not been met, so she is not be-trothed. All she wants is to nullify the transaction.]"

C. Then take note of the case in which there is no such document! [In that case, who brings proof, since he made the condition orally, and now he does not seek to retrieve a document of any sort?]

D. Said R. Yose, "Since he seeks to bar her from marry-ing anyone else, it still is his task to bring proof."

E. [What if] they got married during the time specified by the writ of betrothal? [Is he believed when he says that he has given her what he specified, at the appro-priate time, that is, before he married her?]

F. Such a case came before R. Abbahu. He ruled, "Go, pay."

G. The husband said to him, "Rabbi, [according to your ruling, I never met the stipulated condition, and, ac-cordingly,] I have not even acquired this woman as my wife at all, and yet you tell me, 'Go, pay'?"

H. Said R. Abbahu, "In my whole life, this is the only man who ever made a fool of me."

I. [Abbahu] went and ruled, "If [the husband] retracted, he still must pay, [so he does not have the right to retract] and if the wife retracted, she must pay."

J. Now is this not precisely his ruling at the outset [prior to the man's clever argument]?

K. He treated the matter as a court action. [Since he married her, the stipulation no longer is in effect, but he must carry it out.]

The first case is not conclusive, since the associated litigants are chil-dren of a sage. Whether or not ordinary folk were so meticulous about the law is unclear. Where the principle at hand is subject to court action with Jews not of the rabbinical estate, it involves a claim of mitigating circumstances in a breach of contract. The second case, Abbahu's ruling, by contrast, pertains not to the status of persons but to the requirement that the husband transfer property to the woman. In any event the cases are cited only in the setting of the analysis of legal issues.

This then brings us to the other side of a marriage, its dissolution through divorce or death of the husband. We find ample evidence that rabbinical judges supervised every aspect of the transaction. The procedure according to law involved the delivery of the writ of divorce in the presence of two witnesses, at which point the marriage was deemed severed. The issue of suitable testimony to the act of delivery—the effective act of divorce—had therefore to be worked out. One instance of stories representing rabbinical supervision of the delivery of a writ of divorce is the following.

Y. Qiddushin 3:8.V

> E. Simeon bar Ba brought a writ of divorce and gave it to a woman in the presence of a single witness.
>
> F. The case came before R. Yohanan, who ruled, "A single witness is null in a case involving a married woman.
>
> G. "Did not R. Hiyya bar Assi say in the name of R. Assi, 'A single witness's testimony in the case of a married woman is absolutely worthless'?"

If, further, the writ was brought by messengers, they had to testify that they had witnessed the writing and signing of the writ. In the following cases, that requirement was extended to the transfer of such a writ even within the confines of the area around Caesarea.

Y. Gittin 1:1.VII

> A. R. Eleazar objected to sages [M. Gittin 1:1C], "Just as you maintain [M. Gittin 1:1F]: He who brings a writ of divorce from one province to another overseas has to say, 'In my presence it was written, and in my presence it was signed,' so I maintain that he who brings a writ from one province to another in the Land of Israel has to say, 'In my presence it was written and in my presence it was signed.'"

B. Said R. Jacob bar Zebedi, "There was a case concerning one who brought a writ of divorce from the harbor of Caesarea [to Caesarea]. The case came before R. Abbahu. He ruled, 'Yes, you have to say, "Before me it was written and before me it was signed."' And yet the harbor of Caesarea is not equivalent to Caesarea. [So Eleazar is right.]"

C. Said R. Abin, "It was the case of a ship which was en route."

If the original agent delivering a writ got sick, a court would appoint a replacement. This transaction, too, was supervised, as we should expect, by other courts, which recognized the authority of one another as part of a single system.

Y. Gittin 3:6.II

A. What if the second agent also got sick?

B. Said R. Haninah, son of R. Abba, "Such a case in fact happened, and someone asked and sent to R. Hiyya and to R. Yosa and to R. Immi, and they instructed him, 'The latter agent does not have to say, 'In my presence it was written and in my presence it was signed,' but he merely states, 'I am the agent of a court'" [M. Gittin 3:6DE].

The rabbinical courts carried on a longstanding tradition within Israelite law on the scribal role in preparing writs of divorce. The character of rulings before us suggests that most fundamental questions had been settled long before. In any event, these are matters over which clerks surely had complete control. People assumed they knew what they were doing, and, for its part, the state cannot have taken much interest in the administration of such matters among a subordinate community that had long conducted its own affairs. A minor point such as the following surely fell within sages' power.

Y. Gittin 4:2.V

R. [As to the husband's paying the fee,] it is in line with the following: Doshu, brother of Dodu, was divorcing

his wife. The case came before sages, who ruled that
she must pay the fee of the scribe.

S. And have we not learned: The husband pays the fee
of the scribe?

T. R. Ili in the name of Samuel, "We deal [when the
husband pays the fee] with a case in which the wife
forgives the repayment of her marriage settlement
[in which case the husband enjoys the benefit of the
writ and must pay the fee for preparing it, since he
profits]."

The second means of nullifying a marital bond was through a rite of
halisah, removing the husband's shoe, under the circumstances of a
levirate connection described at Deuteronomy 25:510. The Yerushalmi's
claim that a rabbinical judge administered the law in a given case is
illustrated in the following.

Y. Yebamot 12:6.V

I. A case came before R. Hiyya bar Wawa, and he said to
him, "My son, this woman does not want to be married
to you through a levirate marriage, but perform the
rite of *halisah* with her, and so remove your connection from her, and then she may be married to you
through a normal marriage."

J. After he had performed the rite of *halisah* for her, he
said to him, "If Moses and Samuel should come, she
will not be permitted to you."

K. Concerning [Hiyya, the man] recited this verse,
"They are skilled in doing evil, but how to do good
they know not" (Jeremiah 4:22).

Here, the sage was able to trick the man into severing the levirate
connection to the woman with the promise that, afterward, she would
marry him. The man's ignorance of the law is taken for granted. In this
way the clerk's court was able to prevent a woman from having to marry
someone she did not want.

We come, finally, to instances in which rabbinical courts dealt with
questions of personal status of a rather special character, involving, on
the lower end of the scale, slaves, and, on the upper, wives of priests. In

fact it is our perspective, not that of the Yerushalmi, that encompasses the condition of slaves within the rubric of cases involving personal status. From the perspective of the law, slaves in general are chattels, movable property to be disposed of in an ordinary way. The principle involved in the following case is that, if one loses property, he retains title to it until he despairs of recovering what has been lost. At that point he is deemed to have relinquished title. Exactly that principle, applicable to a cow or a book, pertains to the slave in the following discourse in court.

Y. Gittin 4:4.IV

> N. The slave girl of Rabbah bar Zutra fled. He despaired of recovering her. He came and asked R. Haninah and R. Joshua b. Levi [after getting her back]. He said to him, "He has not got the right to enslave her again."

The conditions in which a person entered slavery were taken into account. It was assumed that when an Israelite sold himself as a slave, it was because he had no choice at all. This was how he would pay his debts or even secure some small means of support. Courts had the power to redeem Jews from slavery through use of communal funds, that is, tax money. Here is one such case.

Y. Gittin 4:9

> A. He who sells himself and his children to a Gentile—
> B. —they do not redeem him, but they do redeem the children after their father's death.

> I. A. The Mishnah [at M. Gittin 4:9AB] speaks of one who repeatedly has sold himself. But if he sold himself for the first time, they do redeem him.
> B. But if he sold himself to Lydians [who are cannibals], then even if it was the first time, they do not redeem him.
> C. Someone sold himself to Lydians. The case came before R. Abbahu. He ruled, "What shall we do? He did it for a living [having no alternative, and he should be redeemed]."

We come, finally, to the determination of the status of a woman as
legitimate wife of a priest. Scripture provides (Leviticus 22:10ff.) that the
household of a priest may eat the holy things given to the priest as his
rations. Nonpriests, by contrast, may not eat such rations. Accordingly,
an important property right was involved in deciding whether a woman
was validly married to a member of the priestly caste, or whether, indeed,
she was permitted to enter into such a marriage. That is why the courts
could rule in matters of personal status such as the following.

Y. Nedarim 11:12.I

> E. Soldiers came into a city, and a woman came and said,
> "Soldiers embraced me and had sexual relations with
> me." Nonetheless [Hananiah] permitted her to eat
> food in the status of heave offering [even though she
> had been raped].
>
> F. The case [of a priest's daughter, not married] came
> before R. Isaac bar Tabelai, concerning a woman who
> said, "My [gentile] stableman seduced me." He said to
> her, "Is not the stableman prohibited?" And he pro-
> hibited her from eating food in the status of heave
> offering.
>
> G. Here [F] you say that he prohibited, and there [E]
> you say that he permitted [her to eat heave offering].
>
> H. There [where she is not believed at all] she came with
> the intent of prohibiting herself, and he declared her
> permitted [not permitting her to get a divorce from
> her husband]. But here she came to permit herself [to
> continue to eat heave offering], so he declared her
> forbidden.

Y. Gittin 9:4.I

> C. A case came before R. Yohanan. It dealt with the wife
> of a priest [and if the writ of divorce were deemed
> valid she could not then go back and live with him].
> He proposed to rule in accord with R. Yannai [that
> the writ was invalid]. When he heard that Rab and
> Samuel differ, when a case came before him involving
> even a mere Israelite, [he would validate the writ].

The matter of personal status predominates in the foregoing case reports. The clerks are represented as exercising their judgment in a rather shrewd way. The law settled little where common sense came into play.

The purpose of this protracted survey of types of case reports of sages acting as judges has now to be briefly restated. The authorities who stood behind the Yerushalmi, in the latter part of the fourth century, preserved a vast number and wide variety of cases in which, so far as they were concerned, rabbinical courts exercised a kind of authority we may regard only as political and bureaucratic. Persons and property of Israel came under their authority. So the Yerushalmi represents its authorities as judges of litigation and administrators of questions of personal status. Decisions are represented, moreover, as precedents, accepted in theorizing about law and uniformly authoritative for courts spread over a considerable territory. Accordingly, rabbinical judges saw themselves as part of a system and a structure, not merely local strongmen or popular sages. A fully articulated system of politics and government, staffed by people who knew the Mishnah and how to apply its law to concrete cases and who had the full power to do so, is represented here. Rabbinical judges knew what to do and had full confidence in their authority to do it.

The Yerushalmi represents the sage not only as a part of a national government and bureaucracy, but also as prefect in his own community. The basis of his authority in this second role was partly the same as with his court role. He could effect judgments bearing significant consequences for the disposition of property, for example, in trade and commerce. But other sorts of decisions shade off into less tangible issues, leading us to a view of the sage as something other than a solely political figure. The same local authority who could settle litigations and direct the course of commerce also could tell people the rules of public fasting. He could give directions for the disposition of synagogue property and the conduct of worship as well, though his presence is scarcely represented as important in the liturgy of the synagogue.

The principal evidence of the character of the sage as a public figure exercising at one and the same time political and religious authority (again, a distinction important now, not then) derives from stories about the sage as the figure mediating between Jews and the outside world. In this context the sage comes forth as head of the Jewish nation in his locale. This is because of his power to represent the nation in its dealings with other groups or to direct Jews on how to conduct those transactions. Whatever the condition of the Jews' government in the country at large (whether, as seems likely, there was a central institution with power over local prefects, for instance), it is in this context that we see the sage as the Big Man (in the anthropological sense) of the Jews. But that portrait emerges from the rabbis' own writings. We do not know how others saw them.

We begin our brief survey of how the sage is represented as local authority with the ways in which he mediated between Israel and the Gentiles of his town. The first, and most important, relationship was with the government. Here the rabbi's power was limited to accommodating the law of the Jews to the demands of the state, so far as that could be done. A striking instance involved the observance of the total cessation of farming, hence, of productive economic activity, every seventh year, that is, the taboo of the Sabbatical Year. If, as was quite natural, the government insisted on the payment of taxes in that year too, then some sort of crop had to be sown. In the following account, Yannai is represented as allowing minimal agricultural labor, along with the rationale for similar sorts of Jewish compromises with the demands of the state.

Y. Sanhedrin 3:5.II

N. When the government first became oppressive, R. Yannai gave instructions that the people might plough one time. There was an apostate to idolatry, who transgressed the laws of the Seventh Year. When he saw them throw up the ploughed clods, he said to them, "Oh! that perversion of the law! You have been given permission to plough [in the Sabbatical Year, because of the government's edict], but have you been permitted to throw up the ploughed clods?"

O. [As to Yannai's permitting the people to plough in the Seventh Year] said R. Jacob bar Zabedi, "I asked before R. Abbahu, 'Did not Zeira and R. Yohanan in the name of R. Yannai say, [or] R. Yohanan in the name of R. Simeon b. Yehosedeq: "They voted in the upper room of the house of Nitzeh in Lud:

P. "'In regard to the Torah, how do we know that if an idolater should tell an Israelite to transgress any one of all of the religious duties which are stated in the Torah, except for idolatry, fornication, and murder, that he should transgress and not be put to death . . . ?

Q. "'Now that rule applies to some matter which is done in private.

R. "'But if it is a matter of public desecration, then even for the most minor religious duty, one should not obey him. [So how could Yannai have permitted the people to plough in the Seventh Year?]"'

S. (For example, there is the case of Papus and Lulianos, his brother, to whom they gave water in a colored glass flask [bearing an idol's name], and they did not accept it from them.)

T. [Yannai] said, "[The case is different here. For] they do not have in mind to force the Jews to commit apostasy [which is not the issue], but solely to pay taxes. [In such a case it is permitted publicly to violate the laws of the Torah.]"

X. R. Yonah and R. Yose gave instructions to bake bread for Ursinicus on the Sabbath.

Y. Said R. Mani, "I asked before R. Jonah, 'Father, now did not R. Zeira, R. Yohanan in the name of R. Yannai, R. Jeremiah, R. Yohanan in the name of R. Simeon b. Yehosedeq say: "They voted in the upper room of the house of Nitzeh, etc. [as above, O-R]." [So how can you permit Jews to bake bread in public on the Sabbath?]'"

Z. He did not intend to force them to apostasize; he intended only to eat warm bread.

UU. When Perocles came to Sepphoris, R. Mana instructed the bakers to put out [bread] in the marketplace on the Sabbath.

VV. Rabbis of Naveh gave instructions [to the bakers] to bake leavened bread on Passover.

What is important in these stories is the implication, taken for granted throughout, that the sage of a locale served as authority not only in municipal court but also in governing relationships with the state. Yet his authority continued to rest solely on his mastery of the law. That is, he could permit actions normally prohibited in the law. He is represented not as negotiating, only as accommodating. Accordingly, so far as the Jewish nation of the Land of Israel was represented in ongoing relationships with the government, some other sort of figure than the sage presumably took charge. Furthermore, the unstated supposition is that Israel stands in a subordinated relationship, able to resist only with difficulty, and then at a very high cost. The alternative to submission is assumed to be death. So the domain over which the sage presided flourished on the edge of an active volcano.

The common-sense distinction expressed in the foregoing stories between accommodating the government's legitimate needs, on the one side, and opposing at all costs its intervention into Israelite faith, on the other, represented sound social policy. The community remained intact. But it also survived its subjugation. At the same time the rabbinical authorities kept at a distance recognition of the naked power of the Gentile. The Romans ruled by law, which Jews would keep. But so far as sages conferred legitimacy, the Gentile could not rule by force, nor intervene in the Jews' everyday life.

Y. Sheqalim 7:2.VI

> D. A man went to buy a piece of meat from a butcher, but he did not give him any. He told a Roman, who brought him meat. He said to him, "Did you not take it from him by force?"
>
> E. He said to him, "And did I not exchange it for a piece of carrion meat?" [Accordingly, the butcher is now deemed unfaithful and may not be patronized.]
>
> F. R. Jeremiah in the name of R. Haninah: "The case came before Rabbi, who ruled, '[The Roman] does not have the power to prohibit Israelites from patronizing all of the butchershops in Sepphoris [by what he may say about the conduct of the owners].'"

In the foregoing story we see once again both the power of the sages and the limits of that power. In mediating between Israel and the threatening world, the sages could control Israel's response, imparting a sense of predictability and governance of their own fate upon which the Jews, for their part, could rely. But what this meant in the present case is that Jews would buy meat from Jewish butchers thrown into suspicion by the Roman's (or Aramaean's) deed.

When the sages could get away with it, on the other hand, they were prepared to prohibit gentile worship and destroy their religious objects. So accommodation was made to what could not be avoided; there never was a question either of accepting gentile rule as legitimate or of extending to Gentiles subject to rabbinical-Israelite authority equivalent toleration.

Y. Abodah Zarah 4:4.IV

A. [With reference to the following passage of the Mishnah: A Gentile has the power to nullify an idol belonging either to himself or his fellow, but an Israelite does not have the power to nullify an idol belonging to a Gentile,] R. Yohanan in the name of R. Yannai derived that view from the following verse of Scripture: "You shall not covet the silver or the gold that is on them or take it for yourselves" (Deuteronomy 7:25). "You may not covet and take [that gold], but others may covet [the gold], and then you may take it."

B. R. Yohanan said to Bar Derosai, "Go, break all the idols that are in the public baths [of Tiberias]," and he went and broke all of them except for one.

C. And why so?

D. Said R. Yosé b. R. Bun, "Because a certain Israelite was suspected of going and offering incense on that one [and an idol worshiped by an Israelite is not subject to nullification at all]."

As to the local Gentiles, they were to be appeased "for the sake of peace." Here too, of course, there would be no question of violating the laws of the Jews. But could one do business on a gentile feast day? Here a local sage gives the answer to that question.

Y. Abodah Zarah 1:3.III

B. The [Israelite] folk of Girda asked R. Ami, "As to the day on which Gentiles make a feast, what is the law [about doing business with them]?"

C. He considered permitting it to them on the grounds of maintaining peace [in relationships].

D. Said to him R. Ba, "And did not R. Hiyya teach: 'On the day of a banquet of Gentiles it is forbidden [to do business with them]'?"

E. Said R. Ami, "Were it not for R. Ba, we should have

> ended up permitting their idolatrous practices. So blessed is the Omnipresent who has kept us distant from them!"

Relationships between Jews and Gentiles were hardly so formal and distant as these tales suggest. Jews and Gentiles lived side by side. It was perfectly natural for daily interaction to lead to mutual hospitality. Accordingly, the issue of Jews eating what Gentiles cooked had to be faced. A subsidiary problem involved wine. The Mishnah's law took for granted that a Gentile would flick a drop of wine as a libation every time he opened a keg. That act rendered the rest of the keg forbidden to Israelite consumption or even benefit, for instance, in trade. The prohibition against wine with which Gentiles had had physical contact extended to the casks or skins, the cups, wine presses and vats, and any other utensils in which that wine had been contained. These considerations appear in stories, told in official and communal settings, about eating food deriving from Gentiles and utilizing utensils in which Gentiles' wine had been kept. The first group of tales takes up food prepared by Gentiles.

Y. Abodah Zarah 2:8.V

> E. A fire [set by a Gentile] broke out in a reed thicket and in a date grove, and there were locusts there, which got roasted. The case then came before R. Mana, who prohibited [Israelites from eating the locusts, because they had been roasted by a Gentile, even though it was not the Gentiles' deliberate action that had led to the locusts being roasted].

Y. Abodah Zarah 2:8.VI

> A. What is the law governing [Israelite consumption of] their [Gentiles'] lupines?
> B. Rabbi prohibits.
> C. Geniba permits.
> D. Said Rabbi, "I am an elder, and he is an elder. I intend to prohibit them, and he intends to permit them."
> E. R. Mana bar Tanhum went to Tyre and permitted [Israelites to make use of] lupines prepared by [Gentiles].

F. R. Hiyya bar Ba went to Tyre and found that R. Mana bar Tanhum had permitted lupines prepared by [Gentiles]. He went to R. Yohanan. [Yohanan] said to him, "What sort of case came to your hand?"

G. He said to him, "I found that R. Mana bar Tanhum had permitted [Israelites to eat] lupines prepared by [Gentiles]."

H. [Yohanan] said to [Hiyya], "And did you punish him [by declaring him to be excommunicated]?"

I. He said to him, "He is a great man, for [so wise is he that] he knows how to sweeten [the water of the] Mediterranean sea."

J. He said to him, "It is not so, my son. He merely knows how to take the measure of the water. For when the water praises God who created it, [the water] turns sweet. [So his knowledge is not so impressive.]"

The first story indicates that a sage was consulted about eating food cooked by Gentiles' inadvertent action. It does not tell us who brought the question or who accepted the answer; we cannot take for granted that ordinary folk, not disciples of sages, were involved. The second tale, by contrast, suggests the rabbi's ruling was accepted by a wide audience of Jews. But neither is probative; we may assume that the Yerushalmi takes for granted popular adherence to rabbinical rulings in these matters.

The rabbi's authority as representative of the Jewish nation and mediator between that nation and the gentile world in general, and the government in particular, bore heavy symbolic weight. But in shaping the Jewish community to accord with "the Torah," the rabbi's local authority outside the court produced far more significant, concrete results. It is at this point that we see the shading off of the character of the rabbi's decisions, as they dealt less with disposition of persons and property and more with intangible matters of proper conduct and observance of religious taboos. These matters, still, presented public and social issues, in which the sage not merely exemplified, but also enforced, law. In the next section we shall see how the sage extended his influence solely through expressing his opinion, as distinct from issuing orders as a public official. But, once again we must remind ourselves, the distinction is ours. The texts before us treat as one all sorts of authority.

A significant rabbinical function, in towns in which sages ruled, was to provide support for the poor by collecting and distributing alms. In these stories we see that the Yerushalmi's framers took for granted that sages carried out this task, expressing in the way they did the work their convictions on relying ultimately on God and on appeasing public opinion.

Y. Ketubot 6:5.I

H. There was the case of a girl who came in the time of R. Ammi. He told her [that she could not have money at that time, since] he had to leave money over [for the poor] for the festival.

I. Said to him R. Zeira, "You are causing a loss to her. But let her take what is in the pot. The Master of the festival is yet alive [God, who will provide]."

Y. Sheqalim 5:4.I

A. R. Jacob bar Idi and R. Isaac bar Nahman were supervisors [of the communal funds.] They would give R. Hama, father of R. Hoshaiah, a denar. He then would divide it among others [who needed it].

B. R. Zechariah, father-in-law of R. Levi, was subject to public slander. People said that he did not have need but he took [charity anyhow]. After he died, they looked into the matter and found that he would divide up [the funds] among others [in need].

C. R. Hinena bar Papa would pass out charity funds by night. One time the lord of the spirits met him. He said to him, "Did not Our Rabbi [Moses] teach us, 'You shall not remove your neighbor's landmark' (Deuteronomy 19:14) [meaning, you should not be out by night, over which I rule]?"

D. He said to him, "Is it not written, 'A gift in secret averts anger; and a bribe in the bosom, strong wrath'?" (Proverbs 21:14).

E. The other stepped back from him and fled.

F. Said R. Jonah, "'Happy is he who gives to the poor' is not written here, but rather, 'Blessed is he who considers the poor' (Psalm 41:1).

G. "This refers to one who examines the religious duty of charity, figuring out how to do it properly."

H. How then did R. Jonah do it?

I. When he saw a poor person, son of worthy parents, who had lost his property, he would say to him, "Since I heard that you have inherited property from some other source, take some money now and pay me back later on."

J. When the poor person would take the money, he would say to him, "It is a gift for you."

These stories do not suggest that the clerk in particular engaged in systematic support of the poor. They are random and individual, bearing slight implication of an ongoing and institutional role. Once again, we are not certain that the clerks in particular did this work to the exclusion of other sorts of Jewish authorities. While sages clearly served as supervisors of communal funds, we have no reason to suppose that all supervisors of communal funds were sages. Accordingly, the sages appear as a kind of caste or estate, but not as the company of everyone involved in the government of the Jewish nation.

Rabbinical authority is represented as extending not only to public observances, but to personal rites as well. Rabbis instructed individuals on the way to carry out duties of a nonprivate character, such as burials. At issue here are decisions on reburial of the deceased; when the rites of mourning, following burial, actually come into effect; and the applicability of rites of mourning to a priest in doubt as to his relationship to the deceased. In all of these instances as in many others, private conduct was deemed subject to public authority, and the sage is represented as the source of rulings on them.

Y. Moed Qatan 3:5.XII

S. Gamaliel of Quntiah was buried by the people of Kursai in their place. After three days they reconsidered the matter [and wished to bury him in his own town]. They came and asked R. Simeon.

T. R. Simeon said to them in the name of R. Joshua b. Levi, "Since you did not give thought to moving him once the burial had taken place, the rites of mourning are counted from the time at which the original grave was sealed."

U. Jeshua, brother of Dorai, had a case. He came and asked R. Abbahu. He said to him, "The rites of mourning commence once the second grave has been sealed."

V. Said to him R. Jacob bar Aha, "I was with you when
    you asked that question to R. Abodema of Haifa, who
    said, 'It is when the first grave has been sealed.'"

Y. Yebamot 11:7.II

C. R. Asian bar Yequm had a case. He asked R. Yosa
    [about how to decide concerning a priest's mourning
    the death of a child who was subject to doubt]. He said
    to him, "You do not have [to undertake the rites of
    mourning in such a case]."

The matter of recognition of legitimate parentage affected a broader
range of issues than that in the preceding instances. If the child was
conceived in a union of a man and woman not permitted by Jewish law to
marry, then the status of the child for diverse purposes had to be
determined. For example, in the following story, the issue is whether or
not the son of a Gentile woman and a Jewish man was deemed an
Israelite and so might be circumcised on the eighth day after birth, even
on the Sabbath day. If the child was a Jew, then the rite of circumcision
was to take place, though this rite required actions otherwise forbidden
on the Sabbath day. The question was brought to a Jewish judge, not
called a sage. Accordingly, someone took for granted that the Jewish
authority had a right to make such a decision. But the consensus of the
sages stood contrary to the authority's ruling. Here we see the parame-
ters of rabbinical authority in the community at large. Where individuals
were involved, sages had a say. Where the community at large possessed
a tradition, sages generally went along with custom, especially if it made
little difference. Over their own functionaries the rabbinical authorities
exercised substantial control.

Y. Yebamot 2:6.III

M. Jacob of Kephar Naborayya went to Tyre. They came
    and asked him, "What is the law as to circumcising
    the son of an Aramaean woman [and a Jewish man]
    on the Sabbath?"
N. He considered permitting them, on the basis of the
    following verse: "[And on the first day of the second
    month, they assembled the whole congregation to-
    gether] who registered themselves by families, by

father's houses, [according to the number or names from twenty years old and upward, head by head]" [Numbers 1:18]. [Hence the child follows the status of the father.]

O. R. Haggai heard and said, "Go and bring him to me, so that he may be flogged."

P. He said to him "On what basis do you flog me?"

Q. He said to him, "It is on the basis of the following verse of Scripture: 'Therefore let us make a covenant with our God [to put away all these wives and their children, according to the counsel of my lord and of those who tremble at the commandment of our God; and let it be done according to the law].'" [Ezra 10:3]

R. He said to him, "On the basis of a mere tradition [and not of a verse of the Torah itself] are you going to have me flogged?"

S. He said to him, "'. . . and let it be done according to the law' (Ezra 10:3)."

T. He said to him, "And on the basis of what verse of Scripture?"

U. He said to him, "It is in line with that which R. Yohanan said in the name of R. Simeon b. Yohai, 'It is written, You shall not make marriages with them, [giving your daughters to their sons or taking their daughters for your sons]' [Deuteronomy 7:3]. And it is written, 'For they would turn away your sons from following me, [to serve other gods; then the anger of the Lord would be kindled against you, and he would destroy you quickly]' [Deuteronomy 7:4]. Your son from an Israelite is called your son, and your son from a Gentile woman is not called your son, but her son."

V. He said to him, "Lay on your flogging, for it will be good to receive [since I have it coming]."

The story need not represent a practical case, since the inquiry concerns abstract law, not a concrete decision. But it makes little difference, for the main point is that rabbinical authorities, hearing such an opinion or decision, took prompt action to correct the error and punish the one who made it. Accordingly, the Yerushalmi takes for granted that the rabbinical group could discipline people who undertook rulings in areas on which "the Torah" had opinions. That the kind of law at hand indeed produced practical precedents is indicated in what now follows.

The stories we have reviewed tell us how the framers of the Yerushalmi wished to portray their own practical position as local authority. They represent the governed as meekly accepting the rulings of the rabbinical governor. Only the subterranean theme that local practice and opinion must come into consideration suggests that rabbinical authority depended, in the end, upon the acquiescence and acceptance of others. Without an explicit account of the workings of the community the foregoing picture remains lifeless—and misleading. Accordingly, we conclude our survey with a story of how local Big Men disposed of the rabbinical Big Man. There can be no doubt that the sage was perceived, and saw himself, as an outsider, someone who came from somewhere else to exercise power, a prefect from on high. Whatever his backing from the patriarch and from Heaven, whatever his qualifications as master of Torah teachings and Torah power, in the end the sage had to secure acceptance based on solid achievement in relating to the local folk and in winning their respect. The point of the story comes at IV.Eff., but the details of the opening part are essential for understanding what follows.

Y. Yebamot 12:6.III

> A. There [in Babylonia, where they prepare a writ of *halisah*], they state in the writ, "She appeared before us and removed his shoe from his right foot and spit before us with spittle which could be seen on the ground [M. Yebamot 12:6H], and she stated, 'So shall it be done to the man who does not build up his brother's house.'"

> IV. A. Said R. Abbahu, "Once the spittle has come out of her mouth, even if the wind picked it up and carried it away, the rite is valid."
>
> B. If she spit blood—
>
> C. R. Ba in the name of R. Judah, R. Zeriqan introduced the statement [in the name of] R. Jeremiah in the name of Abba bar Abba, R. Zeira introduced the matter in the name of Samuel: "If there is any remnant of spittle [in it], it is valid."
>
> D. A woman without hands—how does she remove the shoe? With her teeth.

E. The people of Simonia came before Rabbi. They said to him, "We want you to give us a man to serve as preacher, judge, reader, teacher, and to do all the things we need." He gave them Levi bar Sisi.

F. They set up a great stage and seated him on it. They came and asked him, "A woman without arms—with what does she remove the shoe?" And he did not answer.

G. If she spit blood . . . ?

H. And he did not answer.

I. They said, "Perhaps he is not a master of the law. Let us ask him something about lore." They came and asked him, "What is the meaning of the following verse, as it is written, 'But I will tell you what is inscribed in the book, in truth' (Daniel 10:21). If it is truth, why is it described as inscribed? And if it is inscribed, why is it described as truth?"

J. He did not answer them.

K. They came back to Rabbi and said to him, "Is this a mason of your masons' guild [a pupil of your school]?"

L. He said to them, "By your lives! I gave you someone who is as good as I am."

M. He sent and summoned him and asked him. He said to him, "If the woman spit blood, what is the law?"

N. He answered him, "If there is a drop of spittle in it, it is valid."

O. A woman without arms—how does she remove the shoe?"

P. He said to him, "She removes the shoe with her teeth."

Q. He said to him, "What is the meaning of the following verse, as it is written, 'But I will tell you what is inscribed in the book, in truth' (Daniel 10:21). If it is truth, why is it described as inscribed, and if it is inscribed, why is it described as truth?"

R. He said to him, "Before a decree is sealed, it is described as inscribed. Once it is sealed, it is described as truth."

S. He said to him, "And why did you not answer the people when they asked you these same questions?"

T. He said to him, "They made a great stage and seated me on it, and my heart melted."

U. He recited concerning him the following verse of
   Scripture: "If you have been foolish, exalting yourself,
   or if you have been devising evil, put your hand on
   your mouth' (Proverbs 30:32).

V. "What caused you to make a fool of yourself in regard
   to teachings of Torah? It was because you exalted
   yourself through them."

While the moral of the story is directed to the disciple of a sage, who
is warned not to take pride in the high position to which his learning
may bring him, the setting of the story is important in the present
context. It tells us the Yerushalmi's framers took for granted that important Jewish authorities, not sages, in the end could dispose of a rabbi's
claim to make decisions.

Here once more we see how the sage is marginal to the Jewish
nation in its local life. On the one side, he is on the frontiers of Heaven,
bringing down to the nation the teachings of Heaven. On the other, he is
an outsider to the community, meant to provide for their needs, but also
serving at their pleasure. His standing depends upon what he knows.
But it also depends upon the acceptance of those to whom he teaches and
governs. So the position of the sage as a clerk and a bureaucrat turns out,
in a story such as this one, to be far less secure and established than the
earlier accounts suggested. Harmonizing together the Yerushalmi's diverse pictures of the authority of the sage is hardly necessary; presumably each comes from its own setting and is accurate to that setting. Yet
on balance we do gain a coherent picture of how sages in general
understood the Jewish nation over whom they claimed to rule, and how,
in particular, they saw themselves within that nation. The fact that the
stories portraying that vision also contain dissonant details, pointing
toward a quite different reality from the one imagined by the storytellers,
is hardly surprising.

The sage stood on the intersecting borders of several domains: political and private, communal and individual. He served as both legal and
moral authority, decisor and exemplar, judge and clerk, administrator
and governor, but also holy man and supernatural figure. It is this final
aspect of the sage as public authority that we take up when we turn to
stories about how the sage as a public official was expected to, and did,
perform certain supernatural or magical deeds. These stories place the
sage at the border between heaven and earth, as much as he stood at the
frontier between Israel and the nations: wholly liminal, entirely exem-

plary, at one and the same time. What is important here is the representation of the sage as public authority deemed to exercise supernatural power. These tales are separate from views of the sage as a supernatural figure in general, which we shall review in what follows. In the present setting, the wonder-working sage as a civic figure, in particular, comes to the fore. His task was to use his supernatural power in pretty much the same context and for the same purpose as he used his political-judicial-legal power and learning as well as his local influence and moral authority. Once again we remind ourselves the distinctions are ours, not those of the Yerushalmi, which sees all of these forms of public authority as undifferentiated and of equal consequence.

In the following stories, the responsibility of the sages to stop fires is taken for granted. What is striking is that, in the tales, they exercise that responsibility equally through worldly and otherworldly means: in the first story, by getting Gentiles to do the work; in the second, by using Heaven through calling down rain; in the third, by some sort of merit (not made specific); and in the fourth, by a sage spreading out a cloak, which drives the flames away.

Y. Nedarim 4:9.I

> C. In R. Ami's time there was a fire in town [on the Sabbath]. R. Ami sent out a proclamation in the marketplace of the Aramaeans, saying, "Whoever does the work will not lose out by it." [Ami could not ask the people to do the work, because of the restrictions of the Sabbath on those employed by Israelites. Accordingly, he solved the problem in the way proposed in the present context.] . . .
>
> G. There was a case in which a fire broke out in the courtyard of Yosé b. Simai in Shihin, and the soldiers of the camp of Sepphoris came down to put it out. But he did not let them do so.
>
> H. He said to him, "Let the tax collector come and collect what is owing to him."
>
> I. Forthwith clouds gathered, and rain came and put the fire out. After the Sabbath he sent a sela to every soldier, and to their commander he sent fifty denars.
>
> J. Said R. Hanina, "It was not necessary to do so."
>
> K. There was a Samaritan who was R. Jonah's neighbor.

A fire broke out in the neighborhood of R. Jonah. The Samaritan came and wanted to put it out, but R. Jonah did not let him do so.

L. [The Samaritan] said to him, "Will it be on your responsibility if it burns up my property?"

M. [Jonah] said to him, "Yes." And the whole area was saved.

N. R. Jonah of Kefar Ammi spread out his cloak over the grain, and the flames fled from it.

These several stories show that the sage was seen as bearing responsibility to put out fires, and a mixture of legal subterfuge, supernatural intervention, and sagacity is conveyed in the set of tales. When we call the sage a supernatural authority, what we mean, then, is to indicate that he was a communal official who, on occasion, was believed to invoke more than this-worldly power to carry out his civil duties.

In the following story the sage as public official protects the town from a siege and violence.

Y. Taanit 3:8.II

A. As to Levi ben Sisi: troops came to his town. He took a scroll of the Torah and went up to the roof and said, "Lord of the ages! If a single word of this scroll of the Light has been nullified [in our town], let them come up against us, and if not, let them go their way."

B. Forthwith people went looking for the troops but did not find them [because they had gone their way].

C. A disciple of his did the same thing, and his hand withered, but the troops went their way.

D. A disciple of his disciple did the same thing. His hand did not wither, but they also did not go their way.

E. This illustrates the following apothegm: "You can't insult an idiot, and dead skin doesn't feel the scalpel."

The story is told to make its point, but, once more, it serves to convey a glimpse into the imagination, not merely the morality, of the storyteller and the Yerushalmi's framers. The power of the sage to ward off the siege was based upon his saintliness, which consisted in his obedience to the Torah and the peoples' obedience to him. So whatever public authority the sage exercised is credited, in the end, to his accurate knowledge and sincerity in living up to his own teachings, on the one side, and the peoples' willingness to accept his instructions, on the other.

Earlier we noted that sages made rules on public fasting. For their part, they possessed sufficient merit so that, if they personally fasted, they were supposed to be able to bring rain. Yet another area in which supernatural, as distinct from worldly, authority came to the fore was in preventing epidemics. The first story provides a routine instance of rainmaking; the second, of bringing rain and stopping a pestilence, by two themes being joined together.

Y. Taanit 3:4.V

> A. R. Aha carried out thirteen fasts, and it did not rain. When he went out, a Samaritan met him. [The Samaritan] said to him [to make fun of him], "Rabbi, take off your cloak, because it is going to rain."
>
> B. He said to him, "By the life of that man [you]! Heaven will do a miracle, and this year will prosper, but that man will not live to see it."
>
> C. Heaven did a miracle, and the year prospered, and that Samaritan died.
>
> D. And everybody said, "Come and see the fruit [the man's corpse] [lying in the] sun."

Y. Taanit 3:4.I

> A. There was a pestilence in Sepphoris, but it did not come into the neighborhood in which R. Haninah was living. And the Sepphoreans said, "How is it possible that that elder lives among you, he and his entire neighborhood, in peace, while the town goes to ruin?"
>
> B. [Haninah] went in and said before them, "There was only a single Zimri in his generation, but on his account, twenty-four thousand people died. And in our time, how many Zimris are there in our generation? And yet you are raising a clamor!"
>
> C. One time they had to call a fast, but it did not rain. R. Joshua carried out a fast in the South, and it rained. The Sepphoreans said, "R. Joshua b. Levi brings down rain for the people in the South, but R. Haninah holds back rain for us in Sepphoris."

D. They found it necessary to declare a second time of
    fasting, and sent and summoned R. Joshua b. Levi.
    [Haninah] said to him, "Let my lord go forth with us
    to fast." The two of them went out to fast, but it did
    not rain.

E. He went in and preached to them as follows: "It was
    not R. Joshua b. Levi who brought down rain for the
    people of the South, nor was it R. Haninah who held
    back rain from the people of Sepphoris. But as to the
    Southerners, their hearts are open, and when they
    listen to a teaching of Light [Torah] they submit [to
    accept it], while as to the Sepphoreans, their hearts
    are hard, and when they hear a teaching of Light, they
    do not submit [or accept it]."

F. When he went in, he looked up and saw that the
    [cloudless] air was pure. He said, "Is this how it still
    is? [Is there no change in the weather?]" Forthwith, it
    rained. He took a vow for himself that he would never
    do the same thing again. He said, "How shall I say to
    the creditor [God] not to collect what is owing to
    him."

The tale about Joshua and Haninah is most striking, because it
presents a thoroughly rationalistic picture of the supernatural framework at hand. True, God could do miracles. But if the people caused their
own disasters by not listening to rabbis' Torah teachings, they could
hardly expect God always to forgo imposing the sanction for disobe-
dience, which was holding back rain. Accordingly, there were reliable
laws by which one could deal with the supernatural world that kept
those laws, too. The particular power of the sage was in knowing the law.
The storyteller took for granted, to be sure, that in the end the clerk could
bring rain in a pinch.

The Yerushalmi portrays the sage as an effective authority over Israel.
Yet details of the portrait time and again contradict its main lines. The sage
was part of the administration of a man who stood at the margins of the
rabbinical estate, one foot in, the other out. The sage was further limited in
his power by popular will and consensus, by established custom, and by
other sorts of Jewish Big Men. Furthermore, the sage as clerk and bureaucrat dealt with matters of surpassing triviality, a fair portion of them of no
interest to anyone but a sage, I should imagine. He might decide which dog
a flea might bite. But would the fleas listen to him?

Accordingly, the Yerushalmi's voluminous evidence of rabbis' quest for authority over the Jewish nation, as we review its principal expressions, turns out to present ambiguities about inconsequentialities. On the one hand, the sage could make some practical decisions. On the other, he competed for authority over Israel with the patriarch and with local village heads. And, in general, no Jew decided much. From the viewpoint of the Roman empire, moreover, the sage was apt to have been one among many sorts of invisible men, self-important nonentities, treating as consequential things that concerned no one but themselves, doing little, changing nothing. After all, in the very period in which the tales before us were coming to closure and beginning to constitute the Yerushalmi as we know it, the power of the Jewish nation to govern itself grew ever less. Even the authority of the patriarch supposedly ended within the very period at hand, leaving only sages and their Yerushalmi, legal theory in abundance but legal standing slight indeed. So we discern a certain disproportion between the insistence of the Yerushalmi that sages really decided things and established important precedents, and the Yerushalmi's context—both the actual condition of Israel, whom sages ruled, and the waning authority of the government of Israel, by whom sages were employed. But when we understand the sages' conception of themselves as embodiments of the Torah, this picture becomes entirely comprehensible.

3

The Yerushalmi's Doctrine of the Torah

The Yerushalmi's ultimate concern is to provide Israel with an account of how to overcome the unsatisfactory circumstances of an unredeemed present, so as to accomplish the movement from here to the much-desired future. When the Talmud's authorities present statements on the promise of the law for those who keep it, therefore, they provide glimpses of the goal of the system as a whole. The primacy of the sage, the legitimizing power of the Torah define the Yerushalmi's theory of how Israel is to be saved from its present condition. When we understand the Yerushalmi's doctrine of the Torah and how the sage embodies the Torah, therefore, we also have a clear account of how, in the conception of this Talmud, Israel must so conduct itself as to achieve, or make God want to bring about, salvation.

For the individual salvation meant the life of the world to come, and for the nation, the return to, and restoration of, Jerusalem and its holy Temple. Looking back from the end of the fourth century to the end of the first, the framers of the Talmud surely perceived what two hundred years earlier, with the closure of the Mishnah, need not have appeared obvious and unavoidable, namely, the definitive end of the old order of cultic sanctification. After a hundred years there may have been some doubt. After two centuries more there could have little hope left. The Mishnah had designed a world in which the Temple stood at the center, a society in which the priests presided at the top, and a way of life in which the dominant issue was the sanctification of Israelite life. Whether the full realization of that world, society, and way of life was thought to come sooner or later, the system had been meant only initially as a utopia, but in the end, as a plan and constitution for a material society here in the Land of Israel.

Two hundred years had passed from the closure of the Mishnah to the completion of the Talmud of the Land of Israel. Much had changed. Roman power had receded from part of the world. Pagan rule had given way to the sovereignty of Christian emperors. The old order was cracking; the new order was not yet established. But, from the perspective of Israel, the waiting went on. The interim from Temple to Temple was not differentiated. Whether conditions were less favorable or more favorable hardly made a difference. History stretched backward to a point of disaster, and forward to an unseen and incalculable time beyond the near horizon. Short of supernatural events, salvation was not in sight. Israel for its part lived under its own government, framed within the rules of sanctification, and constituted a holy society. But when would salvation come, and how could people even now hasten that day? These issues, by the nature of things, proved more pressing as the decades rolled by, becoming first one century, then another, while none knew how many more, and how much more, must still be endured.

So the unredeemed state of Israel and the world, the uncertain fate of the individual—these framed and defined the context in which all forms of Judaism necessarily took shape. The question of salvation presented each with a single ineluctable agendum. But it is not merely an axiom generated by our hindsight that makes it necessary to interpret all of a system's answers in the light of the single question of salvation. In the case of the Judaism to which the Yerushalmi attests, the matter is explicitly stated. The final solution to the Jewish problem lay in the Torah: salvation would be attained when Israel kept the Torah fully and completely—in the model of the sage, who even now embodied the Torah.

For the important fact is that Yerushalmi expressly links salvation to keeping the law. This means that the issues of the law were drawn upward into the highest realm of Israelite consciousness. Keeping the law in the right way is represented as not merely right or expedient. It is the way to bring the Messiah, the son of David. This is stated by Levi, as follows:

Y. Taanit 1:1.IX

> X. Said R. Levi, "If Israel would keep a single Sabbath in the proper way, forthwith the son of David would come.
> Y. "What is the Scriptural basis for this view? 'Moses

said, Eat it today, for today is a sabbath to the Lord; today you will not find it in the field' (Exodus 16:25)."

Z. And it says, "For thus said the Lord God, the Holy One of Israel, 'In returning and rest you shall be saved; in quietness and in trust shall be your strength. And you would not wish it'" (Isaiah 30:15).

The coming of the Messiah, moreover, was explicitly linked to the destruction of the Temple. How so? The Messiah was born on the day the Temple was destroyed. Accordingly, as the following story makes explicit, the consolation for the destruction of the Temple lay in the coming of the son of David.

Y. Berakhot 2:3 (translated by Tzvee Zahavy)

A. The rabbis said, "This messiah king if he comes from among the living, David will be his name; if he comes from among the dead, it will be David himself."

B. Said R. Tanhuma, "I say that the Scriptural basis for this teaching is, 'And he shows steadfast love to his messiah, to David and his descendants forever' (Psalm 18:50)."

C. R. Joshua b. Levi said, "Sprout (semah) is his name."

D. R. Yudan, son of R. Aibo, said, "Menahem is his name."

E. Said Hananiah son of R. Abahu, "They do not disagree. The numerical value of the letters of one name equals the numerical value of the other—semah (138) is equal to menahem (138)."

F. And this story supports the view of R. Yudan son of R. Aibo. "Once a Jew was plowing and his ox snorted once before him. An Arab who was passing and heard the sound said to him, 'Jew, loosen your ox and loosen the plow and stop plowing. For today your Temple was destroyed.'

G. "The ox snorted again. He [the Arab] said to him, 'Jew, bind your ox and bind your plow. For today the messiah king was born.' He said to him, 'What is his name?' 'Menahem.' He said to him, 'What is his father's name?' He said to him, 'Hezekiah.' He said to him, 'Where is he from?' He said to him, 'From the royal capital of Bethlehem in Judea.'

H. "He went and sold his ox and sold his plow. And he
became a peddler of infants' felt clothes. And he went
from place to place until he came to that very city. All
of the women bought from him. But Menahem's
mother did not buy from him. He heard the women
saying, 'Menahem's mother, Menahem's mother, come
buy for your child.' She said, 'I want to bring him up to
hate Israel. For on the day he was born, the Temple
was destroyed.' They said to her, 'We are sure that on
this day it was destroyed and on this day it will be
rebuilt.'

I. "She said to him [the peddler], 'I have no money.' He
said to her, 'It is no matter to me. Come and buy for
him and pay me when I return.' A while later he
returned to that city. He said to her, 'How is the
infant doing?' She said to him, 'Since the time you saw
him a wind came and carried him off away from me.'"

These two stories provide a glimpse into a far larger corpus of
theories about the coming of the Messiah. The former, as we have noted,
explicitly links the coming of the Messiah to the proper observance of the
law as sages propound it. From our perspective, that story is the more
important of the two, for by definition it is particular to the matrix in
which our Talmud takes shape. The latter story presents a series of
rather generalized messianic sayings and in no way addresses the distinctive concerns of rabbis and clerks. Yet for that reason it is all the
more important. For in the Mishnah's entire corpus of ideas, there is
scarcely a hint of the paramount idea of the earlier second century, the
hope for the imminent advent of the Messiah. The Mishnah's system,
whole and complete, remains reticent on the entire theme. By contrast,
our Talmud finds ample place for a rich collection of statements on the
messianic theme. What this means is that, between the conclusion of the
Mishnah and the closure of the Talmud, room had been found for
the messianic hope, expressed in images not revised to conform to the
definitive and distinctive traits of the Talmud itself. The two stories
together, therefore, provide ample testimony both to the entry of the
Messiah into the Talmudic structure and to his (if one may use the term)
"rabbinization."

The "rabbinization" of the messianic hope required its neutralization,
so that people's hopes would not be raised prematurely, with consequent,
incalculable damage to the defeated nation. This meant, first of all, that

rabbis insisted the Messiah would come in a process extending over a long period of time, thus not imposing a caesura upon the existence of the nation and disrupting its ordinary life. Accordingly, the Yerushalmi treats the messianic hope as something gradual, to be worked toward, not a sudden cataclysmic event. That conception was fully in accord with the notion that the everyday deeds of people formed a pattern continuous with the salvific history of Israel.

Y. Yoma 3:2.III

A. One time R. Hiyya the Elder and R. Simeon b. Halapta were walking in the valley of Arabel at daybreak. They saw that the light of the morning star was breaking forth. Said R. Hiyya the Elder to R. Simeon b. Halapta, "Son of my master, this is what the redemption of Israel is like—at first, little by little, but in the end it will go along and burst into light.

B. "What is the Scriptural basis for this view? 'Rejoice not over me, O my enemy; when I fall, I shall rise; when I sit in darkness, the Lord will be a light to me' (Micah 7:8).

C. "So, in the beginning, 'When the virgins were gathered together the second time, Mordecai was sitting at the king's gate' (Esther 2:19).

D. "But afterward: 'So Haman took the robes and the horse, and he arrayed Mordecai and made him ride through the open square of the city, proclaiming, Thus shall it be done to the man whom the king delights to honor' (Esther 6:11).

E. "And in the end: 'Then Mordecai went out from the presence of the king in royal robes of blue and white, with a great golden crown and a mantle of fine linen and purple, while the city of Susa shouted and rejoiced' [Esther 8:15].

F. "And finally: 'The Jews had light and gladness and joy and honor'" (Esther 8:16).

We may regard the emphasis upon the slow but steady advent of the Messiah's day as entirely consonant with the notion that the Messiah will come when Israel's condition warrants it. The improvement in standards of observing the Torah, therefore, to be effected by the nation's obedience to the clerks, will serve as a guidepost on the road to redemption. The moral condition of the nation ultimately guarantees salvation. God will respond to Israel's regeneration, planning all the while to save the saved, that is, those who save themselves.

What is most interesting in Yerushalmi's picture is that the hope for the Messiah's coming is further joined to the moral condition of each individual Israelite. Hence the messianic fulfillment was made to depend on the repentance of Israel. The entire drama, envisioned by others in earlier types of Judaism as a world-historical event, was reworked in context into a moment in the life of the individual and the people of Israel collectively. The coming of the Messiah depended not on historical action but on moral regeneration. So from a force that moved Israelites to take up weapons on the battlefield, the messianic hopes and yearnings were transformed into motives for spiritual regeneration and ethical behavior. The energies released in the messianic fervor were then linked to rabbinical government, through which Israel would form the godly society.

Y. Taanit 1:1.IX

J. "'The oracle concerning Dumah. One is calling to me from Seir, "Watchman, what of the night? Watchman, what of the night?" (Isaiah 21:11).'"

K. The Israelites said to Isaiah, "O our Rabbi, Isaiah, What will come for us out of this night?"

L. He said to them, "Wait for me, until I can present the question."

M. Once he had asked the question, he came back to them.

N. They said to him, "Watchman, what of the night? What did the Guardian of the ages tell you?"

O. He said to them, "The watchman says: 'Morning comes; and also the night. If you will inquire, inquire; come back again'" (Isaiah 21:12).

P. They said to him, "Also the night?"

Q. He said to them, "It is not what you are thinking. But there will be morning for the righteous, and night for the wicked, morning for Israel, and night for idolaters."

R. They said to him, "When?"

S. He said to them, "Whenever you want, He too wants [it to be]—if you want it, He wants it."

T. They said to him, "What is standing in the way?"

U. He said to them, "Repentance: 'Come back again'" (Isaiah 21:12).

V. R. Aha in the name of R. Tanhum b. R. Hiyya, "If Israel repents for one day, forthwith the son of David will come.

W. "What is the Scriptural basis? 'If today you would hearken to his voice'" (Psalm 95:7).

When we reflect that the message, "If you want it, He too wants it to be," comes in a generation confronting a dreadful disappointment, its full weight and meaning become clear. The advent of the Messiah will not be heralded by the actions of a pagan king. Whoever relies upon the salvation of a Gentile is going to be disappointed. Israel's salvation depends wholly upon Israel itself.

Two things follow. First, the Jews were made to take up the burden of guilt for their own sorry situation. But, second, they also gained not only responsibility for, but also power over, their fate. They could do something about salvation, just as their sins had brought about their tragedy. This old, familiar message, in no way particular to the Talmud's bureaucrats, took on specificity and concreteness in the context of the Talmud, which offered a rather detailed program for reform and regeneration. The message to a disappointed generation, attracted to the kin-faith, with its now-triumphant messianic fulfillment, and fearful of its own fate in an age of violent attacks upon the synagogue buildings and faithful alike, was stern. But it also promised strength to the weak and hope to the despairing.

No one could be asked to believe that the Messiah would come very soon. The events of the day testified otherwise. So the counsel of the Talmud's sages was patience and consequential deeds. People could not hasten things, but they could do something. The duty of Israel, in the meantime, was to accept the sovereignty of heavenly government.

Y. Sanhedrin 6:9.III

A. R. Abbahu was bereaved. One of his children had passed away from him. R. Jonah and R. Yose went up [to comfort him]. When they called on him, out of reverence for him, they did not express to him a word of Torah. He said to them, "May the rabbis express a word of Torah."

    B. They said to him, "Let our master teach us."

    C. He said to them, "Now if in regard to the government below, in which there is no reliability, [but only] lying, deceit, favoritism, and bribe-taking—

    D. "which is here today and gone tomorrow—

    E. "if concerning that government, it is said, And the relatives of the felon come and inquire after the welfare of the judges and of the witnesses, as if to say, 'We have nothing against you, for you judged honestly' (Y. Sanhedrin 6:9),

    F. "in regard to the government above, in which there is reliability, but no lying, deceit, favoritism, or bribe taking—

    G. "and which endures forever and to all eternity—

    H. "all the more so are we obligated to accept upon ourselves the just decree [of that heavenly government]."

    I. And it says, "That the Lord . . . may show you mercy, and have compassion on you . . ." (Deuteronomy 13:17).

As we shall now see, the heavenly government, revealed in the Torah, was embodied in this world by the figure of the sage. The meaning of the salvific doctrine just outlined becomes fully clear when we uncover the simple fact that the rule of Heaven and the learning and authority of the rabbi on earth turned out to be identified with one another. It follows that salvation for Israel depended upon adherence to the sage and acceptance of his discipline. God's will in Heaven and the sage's words on earth—both constituted Torah. And Israel would be saved through Torah, so the sage was the savior.

The framers of the Talmud regarded "Torah" as the source and guarantor of salvation. But what they understood by the word "Torah" took on meanings particular to the rabbis. They took to heart as salvific acts what others, standing outside of sages' social and mythic framework, would have regarded as routine, or merely hocus pocus. For to the rabbis the principal salvific deed was to "study Torah," by which they meant memorizing Torah sayings by constant repetition, and, as the Talmud itself amply testifies, (for some sages) profound analytic inquiry into the meaning of those sayings. This act of "study of Torah" imparted supernatural power. For example, by repeating words of Torah, the sage could ward off the angel of death and accomplish other miracles as well. So Torah formulas served as incantations. Mastery of Torah transformed the man who engaged in Torah learning into a supernatural figure, able to do things ordinary folk could not do. In the nature of things, the category of "Torah" was vastly expanded so that the symbol of Torah, a Torah scroll, could be compared to a man of Torah, namely, a rabbi. Once it was established that salvation would come from keeping God's will in general, as Israelite holy men had insisted for so many years, it was a small step for rabbis to identify their particular corpus of learning, namely, the Mishnah and associated sayings, with God's will expressed in Scripture, the universally acknowledged revelation. In consequence "Torah" would include pretty much whatever rabbis knew (inclusive of Scripture) and that alone.

Especially striking in the rabbinical doctrine of salvation is the blurring of boundaries between the nation and the individual. Suffering affected both. Catastrophe of an historical and one-time event, such as the destruction of the Temple, was brought into juxtaposition with personal suffering and death. Accordingly, while the things the nation and its people must be saved from were many, the mode of salvation was one. The consequence of the theory of salvation was this: Torah might protect a person from suffering or death, and Torah might in due course save Israel from its subjugation to the nations of the world. In regard to both the individual and society, Torah would save Israel for a life of Torah in Heaven as well as on earth.

Since Heaven was conceived in the model of earth, so that the analysis of traditions on earth corresponded to the discovery of the principles of creation, the full realization of the teachings of Torah on earth, in the life of Israel, would transform Israel into a replica of heaven on earth. We deal, therefore, with a doctrine of salvation in which the operative symbol, namely, Torah, and the determinative deed, namely, Torah learning, defined not only how to reach salvation but also the very nature of the salvation to be attained. The system was whole and cogent. Entering it at any point, we find ourselves at once before the structure as a whole. It is important, then, to recognize, as we do, that the profound issues confronting Israelite existence, national and individual alike, were framed in terms of Torah and resolved through the medium of Torah. Stated simply: Salvation was to come from Torah; the nature of salvation was defined in Torah.

So the single most striking phenomenon, in the matrix of which the Talmud's system of Judaism formed one element, is the vastly expanded definition of the symbol of "Torah." It now was deemed appropriate to compare or apply that symbol to a remarkable range of things. But the principal instance comes first, the claim that a sage (or disciple of a sage)

himself was equivalent to a scroll of the Torah—a material, legal comparison, not merely a symbolic metaphor.

Y. Moed Qatan 3:7.X

> A. He who sees a disciple of a sage who has died is as if
> he sees a scroll of the Torah that has been burned.

Y. Moed Qatan 3:1.XI

> I. R. Jacob bar Abayye in the name of R. Aha: "An elder
> who forgot his learning because of some accident
> which happened to him—they treat him with the
> sanctity owed to an ark [of the Torah]."

In both instances actual behavior was affected. The Talmud of the
Land of Israel (among other rabbinic documents) stretched to the limit
the bounds of the concept of Torah by showing that Scripture itself stood
behind the extension and amplification of divine revelation through
rational inquiry. The processes of reason, very much like those under-
taken in the rabbinical circles of masters and disciples, themselves were
regarded as able to generate Torah teachings, as one thing led to another
through right thinking. Whatever derived from the Torah through sys-
temic logical analysis, that is, Scripture, was part of Torah, that is,
Revelation.

Y. Megillah 1:11.V

> L. R. Abba b. R. Pappi, R. Joshua of Sikhnin in the name
> of R. Levi: "Noah through reflection derived a lesson
> of Torah from another lesson of Torah. He said, 'It has
> been said to me, "And as I gave you the green plants, I
> give you everything" (Genesis 9:3). For what purpose
> has the Scripture used that inclusive phrase? It serves
> to indicate that clean animals are for offerings.'"

Rabbis of course did the same sort of thinking every day. That the
entire corpus of rabbinical learning and tradition belonged to the category of divine revelation was made quite explicit, as in the following.

Y. Sanhedrin 10:1.IV

A. It is written, "Because he has despised the word of the
Lord, [and has broken his commandment, that person
shall be utterly cut off; his iniquity shall be upon
him]" (Numbers 15:31).

B. I know that this applies only when he despised the
teaching of Torah [entirely].

C. How do I know that [this applies] if he denied even a
single verse of Scripture, a single verse of Targum, a
single argument a fortiori?

D. Scripture says, "[Because he has despised the word of
the Lord,] and has broken his commandment, [that
person shall be utterly cut off; his iniquity shall be
upon him]" (Numbers 15:31).

E. As to a single verse of Scripture: "[The sons of Lotan
were Hori and Heman;] and Lotan's sister was
Timna" (Genesis 36:22).

F. As to a single verse of Targum: "Laban called it Je-
garsahadutha: [but Jacob called it Galeed]" (Genesis
31:47).

G. As to a single argument a fortiori: "If Cain is avenged
sevenfold, [truly Lamech, seventy-sevenfold]" (Genesis 4:24).

The notion, moreover, that the sage participated in the work of
revelation, both through his memorizing Torah sayings and through his
reasoning on them, was made explicit. The sage was holy because he
knew Torah. That meant that, in his act of learning Torah, his work of
memorizing and repeating sayings, and his dialectical arguments on the
amplification and analysis of what he learned, the sage took over the
work of Moses in receiving the will of God. This made the sage equivalent
to the prophet, indeed, superior to him. Identifying themselves with a
(mythic) class of "scribes," sages of the Talmud made explicit the superi-
ority of their learning over the direct revelation received by prophets.

Y. Abodah Zarah 2:7.III

D. R. Ishmael repeated the following: "The words of
Torah are subject to prohibition, and they are subject

to remission; they are subject to lenient rulings, and they are subject to strict rulings. But words of scribes all are subject only to strict interpretation, for we have learned there: He who rules, 'There is no requirement to wear phylacteries,' in order to transgress the teachings of the Torah, is exempt. But if he said, 'There are five partitions in the phylactery, instead of four,' in order to add to what the scribes have taught, he is liable'" [M. Sanhedrin 11:3].

E. R. Haninah in the name of R. Idi in the name of R. Tanhum b. R. Hiyya: "More stringent are the words of the elder than the words of the prophets. For it is written, 'Do not preach'—thus they preach—one should not preach of such things (Micah 2:6). And it is written, '[If a man should go about and utter wind and lies, saying,] "I will preach to you of wind and strong drink," he would be the preacher for this people!'" (Micah 2:11).

F. "A prophet and an elder—to what are they comparable? To a king who sent two senators of his to a certain province. Concerning one of them he wrote, 'If he does not show you my seal and signet, do not believe him.' But concerning the other one he wrote, 'Even though he does not show you my seal and signet, believe him.' So in the case of the prophet, he has had to write, 'If a prophet arises among you . . . and gives you a sign or a wonder . . . ' (Deuteronomy 13:1). But here [with regard to an elder:] '. . . according to the instructions which they give you . . . ' (Deuteronomy 17:11) [without a sign or a wonder]."

What is important here is the status imputed by the Talmud to both "words of scribes," and "the elder." Rabbis knew full well they could not provide many signs or wonders. (As we shall see, that did not prevent them from claiming to do just that.) Their principal validation lay in their role as masters of the law and clerks of the bureaucracy. So, they maintained, these attainments and tasks enjoyed a status still higher than that accorded to the written Torah and the prophets. We may hardly be surprised, therefore, that in some sayings sages regarded study of Torah as more important than acts of loving-kindness or other sorts of ethical actions. The master of Torah was then irreplaceable.

Y. Hagigah 1:7.IV

A. When R. Judah would see a deceased person or a bride being praised, he would set his eyes on the disciples and say, "Deeds come before learning. [The students should go after the crowd to praise the dead or the bride, for doing so is a religious duty.]"

B. They voted in the upper room of the house of Aris: "Learning comes before deeds."

C. R. Abbahu was in Caesarea. He sent R. Haninah, his son, to study Torah in Tiberias. They sent and told him, "He is doing deeds of kindness [burying the dead] there [and not studying]."

D. He sent and wrote to him, "Is it because there are no graves in Caesarea that I sent you to Tiberias [to go around burying people]? And they have in fact taken a vote in the upper room of the house of Aris in Lud: 'Studying Torah takes precedence over deeds.'"

E. Rabbis of Caesarea say, "That which you say applies to a case in which there is someone else who can do the deeds which are required. But if there is no one else available to do the required deeds, then doing the religious deed takes precedence over study of Torah."

F. Once R. Hiyya, R. Yosa, R. Ammi were late in coming to see R. Eleazar. He said to them, "Where were you today?"

G. They said to him, "We had to do a religious duty."

H. He said to them, "And were there no others available to do it?"

I. They said to him, "He was an alien in the country, and had no one else to bury him, [his relatives being overseas]."

The issue of the relative importance of good deeds over studying Torah was not a matter of pure theory. Concrete deeds were involved, since a disciple who went off to bury a corpse could not then spend the time reciting his sentences of the Mishnah. Only special circumstances could justify a sage's doing what less important folk could be relied upon to carry out. It must follow that we deal not with ephemeral sayings about the relative merit of one thing over something else, but with declarations of norms. These declarations take us into the center of the

Talmud's system and show us, in progression, how from the hope for messianic salvation, realized in Torah, the system moves on to the centrality of learning in Torah and the critical importance of the rabbi in the salvific process.

Y. Berakhot 2:7 (translated by Tzvee Zahavy)

When R. Simon bar Zebid died, R. Ilia came up and in regard to him expounded as follows, "Four things are essential for the world. But if they are lost they can be replaced [as we see in the following verse]. 'Surely there is a mine for silver, and a place for gold which they refine. Iron is taken out of the earth, and copper is smelted from the ore' (Job 28:12). If these are lost they can be replaced.

"But if a disciple of the sages dies who shall bring us his replacement? Who shall bring us his exchange? 'But where shall wisdom be found and where is the place of understanding?' (Job 28:12) 'It is hid from the eyes of all living' (Job 28:21)."

The sage as master of the Torah held in his hand the power to bring salvation to Israel. Torah as he taught it was the source of Israel's salvation. The supernatural power imputed to him even now was a foretaste of what would come when all Israel conformed to the Torah as the sage taught it. So, as I have insisted, tales of the supernatural or magical power of the rabbi have to be read in the larger setting of the salvific process posited by the Talmud's framers.

It was an axiom of all forms of Judaism that, because Israel had sinned, it was punished by being given over into the hands of earthly empires; when it atoned, it was, and again would be, removed from their power. The means of atonement, reconciliation with God, were specified elsewhere as study of Torah, practice of commandments, and doing good deeds. Why so? The answer is distinctive to the matrix of our Talmud: When Jews in general had mastered Torah, they would become rabbis, just as some now had become rabbis, saints, or holy men. When all Jews had become rabbis, they would no longer lie within the power of the nations, that is, of history. Then the Messiah would come. Redemption then depended upon all Israel's accepting the yoke of the Torah. Why so? Because at that point all Israel would attain a full and complete embodiment of Torah, revelation. Thus conforming to God's will and replicating Heaven, Israel on earth, as a righteous, holy community, would exercise the supernatural power of Torah. They would be able as a whole to do what some few saintly rabbis could do. With access to supernatural power, redemption would naturally follow.

As I have stressed, the theory of salvation focused upon Torah addressed the circumstance of the individual as much as of the nation. This was possible because the same factor had caused the condition of both, namely sin. Not doing the will of God led to the fall of Israel, the destruction of the Temple. Disobediance to the will of God, that is, sin, is what causes people to suffer and die. The angel of death has power, specifically, over those not engaged in the study of Torah and performing of commandments.

This view is expressed in stories indicating the belief that while a sage is repeating Torah sayings, the angel of death cannot approach him.

Y. Moed Qatan 3:5.XXI

F. [Proving that while one is studying Torah, the angel of death cannot touch a person, the following is told:] A disciple of R. Hisda fell sick. He sent two disciples to him, so that they would repeat Mishnah-traditions with him. [The angel of death] turned himself before them into the figure of a snake, and they stopped repeating traditions, and [the sick man] died.

G. A disciple of Bar Pedaiah fell ill. He sent to him two disciples to repeat Mishnah-traditions with him. [The angel of death] turned himself before them into a kind of star, and they stopped repeating Mishnah-traditions, and he died.

Repeating Mishnah-traditions thus warded off death. It is hardly surprising that stories were told about wonders associated with the deaths of various rabbis. These validated the claim of supernatural power imputed to the rabbis. A repertoire of such stories includes two types. First, there is a list of supernatural occurrences accompanying sages' deaths, as in the following.

Y. Abodah Zarah 3:1.II

A. When R. Aha died, a star appeared at noon.

B. When R. Hanah died, the statues bowed down.

C. When R. Yohanan died, the icons bowed down.

D. They said that [this was to indicate] there were no icons like him [so beautiful as Yohanan himself].

E. When R. Hanina of Bet Hauran died, the Sea of Tiberias split open.

F. They said that [this was to commemorate the miracle that took place] when he went up to intercalate the year, and the sea split open before him.

G. When R. Hoshaiah died, the palm of Tiberias fell down.

H. When R. Isaac b. Elisheb died, seventy [infirm] thresholds of houses in Galilee were shaken down.

I. They said that [this was to commemorate the fact that] they [were shaky and] had depended on his merit [for the miracle that permitted them to continue to stand].

J. When R. Samuel bar R. Isaac died, cedars of the land of Israel were uprooted.

K. They said that [this was to take note of the fact that] he would take a branch [of a cedar] and [dance, so] praising a bride [at her wedding, and thereby giving her happiness].

L. The rabbis would ridicule them [for lowering himself by doing so]. Said to them R. Zeira, "Leave him be. Does the old man not know what he is doing?"

M. When he died, a flame came forth from heaven and intervened between his bier and the congregation. For three hours there were voices and thunderings in the world: "Come and see what a sprig of cedar has done for this old man!"

N. [Further] an echo came forth and said, "Woe that Samuel b. R. R. Isaac has died, the doer of merciful deeds."

O. When R. Yosa bar Halputa died, the gutters ran with blood in Laodicea.

P. They said [that the reason was] that he had given his life for the rite of circumcision.

Q. When R. Abbahu died, the pillars of Caesarea wept.

R. The [Gentiles] said [that the reason was] that [the pillars] were celebrating. The Israelites said to them, "And do those who are distant [such as yourselves] know why those who are near [we ourselves] are raising a cry?"

Y. Abodah Zarah 3:1.II

BB. One of the members of the patriarchate died, and
the [burial] cave folded over [and received the bier],
so endangering the lives [of those who had come to
bury him]. R. Yose went up and took leave [of the
deceased], saying "Happy is a man who has left this
world in peace."

CC. When R. Yosa died, the castle of Tiberias collapsed,
and members of the patriarchate were rejoicing.
R. Zeira said to them, "There is no similarity [be-
tween this case and the miracle described at BB].
The peoples' lives were endangered, here no one's
life was endangered. In that case, no pagan worship
was removed, while here, an idol was uprooted [so,
consequently, the event described in BB was not a
miracle, while the event described here was a miracle and a sign of divine favor]."

What is important in the foregoing anthology is the link between the
holy deeds of the sages and the miracles done at their demise. The sages'
merit, attained through study of Torah or through acts of saintliness and
humility (despite mastery of Torah), was demonstrated for all to see. So
the sage was not merely a master of Torah, but his mastery of Torah laid
the foundations for all the other things he was.

It is hardly in the context only of death scenes that miracles were
imputed to rabbis. Their power was compared to that of other wonder-
workers. Rabbis were shown more effective than other magicians, specifically in those very same settings in which, all parties conceded, other
wonder-workers, as much as rabbis, were able to perform magical deeds.
What is important in the following is the fact that, in a contest between a
rabbi and another sort of magician, an Israelite heretic, the rabbi was
shown to enjoy superior magical power.

Y. Sanhedrin 7:12.III

A. When R. Eleazar, R. Joshua, and R. Aqiba went in to
bathe in the baths of Tiberias, a min saw them. He
said what he said, and the arched chamber in the bath
[where idolatrous statues were put up] held them
fast, [so that they could not move].

B. Said R. Eleazar to R. Joshua, "Now Joshua b. Haninah, see what you can do."

C. When that min tried to leave, R. Joshua said what he said, and the doorway of the bath seized and held the min firm, so that whoever went in had to give him a knock [to push by], and whoever went out had to give him a knock [to push by].

D. He said to them, "Undo whatever you have done [to let me go]."

E. They said to him, "Release us, and we shall release you."

F. They released one another.

G. Once they got outside, said R. Joshua to that min, "Lo, you have learned [from us whatever you are going to learn]."

H. He said, "Let's go down to the sea."

I. When they got down to the sea, that min said whatever it was that he said, and the sea split open.

J. He said to them, "Now is this not what Moses, your rabbi, did at the sea?"

K. They said to him, "Do you not concede to us that Moses, our rabbi, walked through it?"

L. He said to them, "Yes."

M. They said to him, "Then walk through it."

N. He walked through it.

O. R. Joshua instructed the ruler of the sea, who swallowed him up.

IV. A. When R. Eliezer, R. Joshua, and Rabban Gamaliel went up to Rome, they came to a certain place and found children making little piles [of dirt]. They said, "Children of the Land of Israel make this sort of thing, and they say, 'This is heave offering,' and 'That is tithe.' It's likely that there are Jews here."

B. They came into one place and were received there.

C. When they sat down to eat, [they noticed] that each dish which they brought into them would first be brought into a small room, and then would be brought to them, and they wondered whether they might be eating sacrifices offered to the dead. [That is, before the food was brought to them, it was brought into a small chamber, in which, they suspected, sacrifices were taken from each dish and offered to an idol.]

D. They said to [the host], "What is your purpose, in the fact that, as to every dish which you bring before us, if you do not bring it first into a small room, you do not bring it in to us?"

E. He said to them, "I have a very old father, and he has made a decree for himself that he will never go out of that small room until he will see the sages of Israel."

F. They said to him, "Go and tell him, 'Come out here to them, for they are here.'"

G. He came out to them.

H. They said to him, "Why do you do this?"

I. He said to them, "Pray for my son, for he has not produced a child."

J. Said R. Eliezer to R. Joshua, "Now, Joshua b. Hananiah, let us see what you will do."

K. He said to them, "Bring me flax seeds," and they brought him flax seeds.

L. He appeared to sow the seed on the table; he appeared to scatter the seed; he appeared to bring the seed up; he appeared to take hold of it, until he drew up a woman, holding on to her tresses.

M. He said to her, "Release whatever [magic] you have done [to this man]."

N. She said to him, "I am not going to release [my spell]."

O. He said to her, "If you don't do it, I shall publicize your [magical secrets]."

P. She said to him, "I cannot do it, for [the magical materials] have been cast into the sea."

Q. R. Joshua made a decree that the sea release [the magical materials] and they came up.

R. They prayed for [the host], and he had the merit of begetting a son, R. Judah b. Bathera.

S. They said, "If we came up here only for the purpose of begetting that righteous man, it would have been enough for us."

T. Said R. Joshua b. Haniniah, "I can take cucumbers and pumpkins and turn them into rams and hosts of rams, and they will produce still more."

These long extracts leave no doubt that the Talmud imputed to
Israel's sages precisely the powers generally assigned to magicians.
There was no important distinction between the one and the other. We
see no claim that the superior merit of the rabbi, based on his knowledge
of Torah, accounted for his remarkable magical power. On the contrary,
the sage did precisely what the magician did, only he did it better. When
the magician then pretended to do what Moses had done, it was his end.
The story about Joshua's magic in Rome is similar, in its explicit reference to sympathetic magic, KL. The result was the discovery that the
childless man had been subject to a spell. There can be no doubt that
distinctions between magic and supernatural power meant nothing to
the Talmud's storytellers. The clerks were not merely holy men; they
were a particular kind of holy men.

In consequence of the belief that rabbis had magical powers, it was
quite natural to impute to rabbis the ability both to bless those who
favored them and to curse those who did not. As to the latter:

Y. Sanhedrin 10:2.VII

II.   Said R. Yose, "This is in line with what the proverb
        says: A person has to scruple about the curse of a
        great master, even if it was for nought."

Y. Abodah Zarah 2:2.IV

I. A snake bit Eleazar b. Dama. He came to Jacob of
   Kefar Sama for healing. Said to [Ben Dama] R. Ishmael, "You have no right to do so, Ben Dama."
J. He said to him, "I shall bring proof that it is permitted
   for him to heal me."
K. But he did not suffice to bring proof before he
   dropped dead.
L. Said to him R. Ishmael, "Happy are you, O Ben Dama,
   for you left this world in peace and did not break
   through the fence of the sages, and so in dying you
   have carried out that which has been said: 'A serpent
   will bite him who breaks through a wall' (Kohelet
   10:8)."

So much for a curse. As to the power of rabbis to impart a blessing, it
was represented in a more subtle way.

It was not merely that rabbis themselves could do magical deeds. Heaven itself would intervene in favor of people who did good to rabbis, even though rabbis, for their part, did nothing. The next story shows how magic was done in behalf of a man and his wife who gave generous support to rabbis, even though the beneficiaries themselves are not represented as participating in the miracle done for their friend.

Y. Horayot 3:4.III

A. R. Eliezer, R. Joshua, R. Akiva went up to Holat Antokhiya in a connection with collecting funds for sages.

B. Now there was a certain man there, by the name of Abba Judah. He would fulfill the commandment [of supporting the sages] in a liberal spirit. One time he lost all his money, and he saw our rabbis and despaired [of helping them]. He went home, and his face was filled with suffering.

C. His wife said to him, "Why is your face filled with suffering?"

D. He said to her, "Our rabbis are here, and I simply do not know what I can do for them."

E. His wife, who was even more righteous than he, said to him, "You have a single field left. Go and sell half of it and give the proceeds to them . . ."

F. He went and did just that. He came to our rabbis, and he gave them the proceeds.

G. Our rabbis prayed in his behalf. They said to him, "Abba Judah, may the Holy One, blessed be He, make up all the things you lack."

H. When they went their way, he went down to plough the half-field that remained in his possession. Now while he was ploughing in the half-field that remained to him, his cow fell and broke a leg. He went down to bring her up, and the Holy One, blessed be He, opened his eyes, and he found a jewel. He said, "It was for my own good that my cow broke its leg."

I. Now when our rabbis returned, they asked about him. They said, "How are things with Abba Judah?"

J. People replied, "Who can [even] gaze upon the face of Abba Judah—Abba Judah of the oxen! Abba Judah of

the camels! Abba Judah of the asses!" So Abba Judah
had returned to his former wealth.

K. Now he came to our rabbis and asked after their
welfare.

L. They said to him, "How is Abba Judah doing?"

M. He said to them, "Your prayer in my behalf has
yielded fruit and more fruit." They said to him, "Even
though to begin with other people gave more than you
did, you were the one whom he wrote down at the top
of the register."

N. They took and seated him with themselves, and they
pronounced upon him the following Scriptural verse:
"A man's gift makes room for him and brings him
before great men" (Proverbs 18:16).

The story takes for granted that the one whose name is at the top of
the rabbis' register of donors is the most blessed on the list. Its emphasis
upon the sure reward for those who contribute to the support of masters
and their disciples only restates the point of that minor detail. Those who
disobey rabbis are cursed and die; those who give them money are blessed
and get rich. This same point is made explicit in the following.

Y. Sotah 7:4.IV

F. R. Aha in the name of R. Tanhum b. R. Hiyya: "If one
has learned, taught, kept, and carried out [the Torah],
and has ample means in his possession to strengthen
the Torah and has not done so, lo, such a one still is in
the category of those who are cursed." [The meaning
of "strengthen" here is to support the masters of the
Torah.]

G. R. Jeremiah in the name of R. Hiyya bar Ba, "[If] one
did not learn, teach, keep, and carry out [the teachings
of the Torah], and did not have ample means to
strengthen [the masters of the Torah] [but nonetheless did strengthen them], lo, such a one falls into the
category of those who are blessed."

H. And R. Hannah, R. Jeremiah in the name of R. Hiyya:
"The Holy One, blessed be He, is going to prepare a
protection for those who carry out religious duties [of

support for masters of Torah] through the protection afforded to the masters of Torah [themselves].

I. "What is the Scriptural basis for that statement? 'For the protection of wisdom is like the protection of money'" (Kohelet 7:12).

J. "And it says, '[The Torah] is a tree of life to those who grasp it; those who hold it fast are called happy'" (Proverbs 3:18).

Thus far we have shown that the Talmud maintains the sage exercised magical/supernatural powers and could reward his friends and punish his enemies. We have now to show that the supernatural status accorded to the person of the sage endowed his deeds with normative, therefore revelatory power. What the sage did had the status of law; the sage was the model of the law, thus the human embodiment of the Torah. That mundane view has to be joined to the otherworldly notion, just now illustrated, that the sage was a holy man. For what made the sage distinctive was his combination of worldly authority and power and otherworldly influence. In the Talmud's view, the clerk in the court and the holy man on the rooftop were one and the same. Given the fundamental point of insistence of the Talmud that the salvation of Israel will derive from keeping the law, the Talmud had no choice but to preserve the tight union between salvation and law, the magical power of the sage and his law-giving authority. We turn now to spell out this definitive trait of the system as a whole, as it is exemplified in the Yerushalmi. To state matters simply: If the sage exercised supernatural power as a kind of living Torah, his very deeds served to reveal law, as much as his word expressed revelation.

The capacity of the sage himself to participate in the process of revelation is illustrated in two types of materials. First of all, tales told about rabbis' behavior on specific occasions immediately are translated into rules for the entire community to keep. Accordingly, he was a source not merely of good example but of prescriptive law.

Y. Abodah Zarah 5:4.III

X. R. Aha went to Emmaus, and he ate dumpling [prepared by Samaritans].

Y. R. Jeremiah ate leavened bread prepared by them.

Z. R. Hezekiah ate their locusts prepared by them.

> AA. R. Abbahu prohibited Israelite use of wine prepared
> by them.

These reports of what rabbis had done enjoyed the same authority, as
the laws on eating what Samaritans cooked, as did citations of traditions in
the names of the great authorities of old or of the day. What someone did
served as a norm, if the person was a sage of sufficient standing.

Far more common in the Talmud are instances in which the deed of a
rabbi is adduced as an authoritative precedent for the law under discussion. It was taken for granted that what a rabbi did, he did because of his
mastery of the law. Even though a formulation of the law was not in
hand, a tale about what a rabbi actually did constituted adequate evidence
on how to formulate the law itself. So from the practice of an authority, a
law might be framed quite independent of the sage. The sage then
functioned as a lawgiver, like Moses. Among many instances of that
mode of generating law are the following.

Y. Abodah Zarah 3:11.II

> A. Gamaliel Zuga was walking along, leaning on the
> shoulder of R. Simeon b. Laqish. They came across an
> image.
> B. He said to him, "What is the law as to passing before
> it?"
> C. He said to him, "Pass before it, but close [your] eyes."
> D. R. Isaac was walking along, leaning on the shoulder of
> R. Yohanan. They came across an idol before the
> council building.
> E. He said to him, "What is the law as to passing before
> it?"
> F. He said to him, "Pass before it, but close [your] eyes."
> G. R. Jacob bar Idi was walking along, leaning upon
> R. Joshua b. Levi. They came across a procession in
> which an idol was carried. He said to him, "Nahum,
> the most holy man, passed before this idol, and will
> you not pass by it? Pass before it but close your eyes."

Y. Abodah Zarah 2:2.III

> FF. R. Aha had chills and fever. [They brought him] a
> medicinal drink prepared from the phallus of

Dionysian revelers. But he would not drink it. They brought it to R. Jonah, and he did drink it. Said R. Mana, "Now if R. Jonah, the patriarch, had known what it was, he would never have drunk it."

GG. Said R. Huna, "That is to say, 'They do not accept healing from something that derives from an act of fornication.'"

What is important is GG, the restatement of the story as a law. The example of a rabbi served to teach how one should live a truly holy life. The requirements went far beyond the measure of the law, extending to refraining from deeds of a most commonplace sort. The example of rabbinical virtue, moreover, was adduced explicitly to account for the supernatural or magical power of a rabbi. There was no doubt, in people's imagination, therefore, that the reason rabbis could do the amazing things people said they did was that they embodied the law and exercised its supernatural or magical power. This is stated quite openly in what follows.

Y. Taanit 3:11.IV

C. There was a house that was about to collapse over there [in Babylonia], and Rab set one of his disciples in the house, until they had cleared out everything from the house. When the disciple left the house, the house collapsed.

D. And there are those who say that it was R. Adda bar Ahwah.

E. Sages sent and said to him, "What sort of good deeds are to your credit [that you have that much merit]?"

F. He said to them, "In my whole life no man ever got to the synagogue in the morning before I did. I never left anybody there when I went out. I never walked four cubits without speaking words of Torah. Nor did I ever mention teachings of Torah in an inappropriate setting. I never laid out a bed and slept for a regular period of time. I never took great strides among the associates. I never called my fellow by a nickname. I never rejoiced in the embarrassment of my fellow. I never cursed my fellow when I was lying by myself in bed. I never walked over in the marketplace to someone who owed me money.

G. "In my entire life I never lost my temper in my household."

H. This was meant to carry out that which is stated as follows: "I will give heed to the way that is blameless. Oh when wilt thou come to me? I will walk with integrity of heart within my house" (Psalm 101:2).

The correlation between learning and teaching, on the one side, and supernatural power or recognition, on the other, is explicit in the following.

Y. Ketubot 12:3.VII

A. R. Yosa fasted eighty fasts in order to see R. Hiyya the Elder [in a dream]. He finally saw him, and his hands trembled and his eyes grew dim.

B. Now if you say that R. Yosa was an unimportant man, [and so was unworthy of such a vision, that is not the case]. For a weaver came before R. Yohanan. He said to him, "I saw in my dream that the heaven fell, and one of your disciples was holding it up."

C. He said to him, "Will you know him [when you see him]?"

D. He said to him, "When I see him, I shall know him." Then all of his disciples passed before him, and he recognized R. Yosa.

E. R. Simeon b. Laqish fasted three hundred fasts in order to have a vision of R. Hiyya the Elder, but he did not see him.

F. Finally he began to be distressed about the matter. He said, "Did he labor in learning of Torah more than I?"

G. They said to him, "He brought Torah to the people of Israel to a greater extent than you have, and not only so, but he even went into exile [to teach on a wider front]."

H. He said to them, "And did I not go into exile too?"

I. They said to him, "You went into exile only to learn, but he went into exile to each others."

This story shows that the storyteller regarded as a fact of life the correlation between mastery of Torah sayings and supernatural power—

visions of the deceased, in this case. That is why Simeon b. Laqish complained, E-F, that he had learned as much Torah as the other, and so had every right to be able to conjure the dead. The greater supernatural power of the other then was explained in terms of the latter's superior service to Torah. It seems to me pointless to distinguish supernatural power from magic. The upshot is that the sage was made a magician by Torah learning and could save Israel through Torah, source of the most powerful magic of all.

As noted above, the special position of the sage as supernaturally-favored figure also imposed on Israelite society the requirement to accord him special dignity. The disciple of a sage himself had to exemplify what was required by his behavior toward his own master, who taught him Torah. The disciple's acts of respect for the master, devotion to his standing and honor, ongoing concern for his comfort were principal expressions of the respect for Torah upon which the entire system rested. Accordingly, the respect paid to the Torah also was due to the sage, a view quite natural in light of the established identification of sage and Torah. In the context of this kind of Judaism, the act of respect paid to a sage transcended merely social and conventional bounds. What may look to us like sycophancy was understood as a religious deed to which Heaven would respond. What was rightly done to a sage produced a Heavenly blessing, and predictably, what was wrongly done, a curse.

Y. Sheqalim 5:4.I

> U. The teacher of the son of R. Hoshaiah the Elder was blind, and he was accustomed to eat with him every day. One day he had guests, and he did not come to eat with him in the evening. He came to him, saying to him, "May my master not be angry with me, for I had guests today, and I thought that I would not allow my master's honor to be cheapened today, so I did not eat with my master today."
>
> V. He said to him, "You have thereby appeased one who is seen but does not see. May the one who sees but is not seen accept your excuse."
>
> W. He said to him, "Whence did you learn this [saying]?"
>
> X. He said to him, "From R. Eliezer b. Jacob. For to the town of R. Eliezer b. Jacob a blind man came. R. Eliezer b. Jacob sat below him, so that people would say, 'If it were not that this man was a great

man, R. Eliezer b. Jacob would not have seated himself lower than he.' They paid the blind man great
honor [and supplied his needs]. The blind man asked,
'Why thus?' They said to him, 'R. Eliezer b. Jacob sat
below you.'

Y.   "So the blind man prayed this prayer: 'You have dealt
faithfully with one who is seen but does not see. May
he who sees but is not seen deal faithfully with you.'"

Special courtesy between sage and disciple, in particular, was
mutual. The disciple honored the sage as he honored his father, and the
sage treated the disciple as his son. This mythic transformation of
ordinary relationships found full expression, in particular, in rites of
mourning and burial, in which the disciple was expected to conduct
himself just as he would if his father had died.

Y. Baba Mesia 2:11.I

G.   A certain man started Rab off in his studies, and
when Rab heard that he had died, he tore his garment
on his account [as a sign of mourning, even though
Rab had studied with him only at the elementary
phase of his education].

H.   R. Yohanan was going up from Tiberias to Sepphoris.
He saw someone coming down from there. He said to
him, "What do you hear in town [in Sepphoris]?"

I.   He said to him, "A rabbi has died, and everyone in
town is running about arranging for his burial."

J.   R. Yohanan knew that it was R. Hanina. So he sent
and brought his best Sabbath garments and tore them
[as a sign of mourning].

K.   Now has it not been taught: Any act of tearing which
is not done at the moment of most intense grief is not
a valid act of tearing [in mourning]? [It must be
spontaneous.]

L.   R. Yohanan wanted to do it in a big way, because
[Hanina had been his master, and he honored him.]

M.   Nonetheless, we still do not know whether R. Yohanan did it this way because he had been his master, or
because it was simply bad news [that the head of the
court had died, and even if Hanina had not been his

master, Yohanan would have behaved in the same way].

N. From the following story about R. Hiyya bar Wa in Sepphoris [we find the answer]. [Hiyya] saw everyone running about. He said, "Why is everyone running about?"

O. They said to him, "R. Yohanan is in session and expounding [Torah] in the schoolhouse of R. Benaiah, and everyone is running to hear him."

P. [Hiyya, who had been Yohanan's principal master, said,] "Blessed is the All-Merciful, who allowed me to see everyone running to hear [my disciple, Yohanan], while I am yet alive." [This indicates that Yohanan, for his part, had studied principally not with Hanina but with Hiyya, as we shall now see.]

Q. "Now I have taught him [all] matters of aggadah, except for Proverbs and Kohelet."

R. This indicates that one [must tear his garment in mourning] for each encounter of discipleship [with a teacher, not merely with the principal teacher]. [Consequently, Yohanan is not in accord with Judah. He tore his garments at Hanina's death because of the bad news that the head of the Sephhoris court had died, not because Hanina had been his principal teacher.]

The sage's relationship with Gentiles and nature were subject to supernatural intervention. So all things acknowledged the sage's special position in the larger scheme of things. The sage's disciples entered into an unnatural relationship with him, as if he were their father. This notion is carried to the extreme view that even if one has studied only a trivial part of his education with a sage, when that man dies, the one-time disciple must go into mourning. Gentile officials, likewise, are represented as paying respect to the sage, the ultimate cachet in a subordinated community. It showed that the sage had attained remarkable status in the world. The gentile rulers thereby conceded two things. First, what the sage knew was of the highest consequence. Second, the sage himself was an angelic or supernatural figure. In all of these ways God's favor was shown to the sage.

In the mind of the sage, the community's institutions existed for the benefit of sages and disciples. The special status of the rabbinical estate was to be recognized, in particular, in synagogues. That was not a matter of special role in the rites as we noted, but involved extraordinary privileges in use of the sacred property. Sages owned the Torah, so they claimed dominion over the synagogue as well. This claim extended far beyond the right of a judge to dispose of communal property.

Y. Megillah 3:3.V

> A. R. Joshua b. Levi said, "Synagogues and schoolhouses belong to sages and their disciples."
>
> B. R. Hiyya bar Yose received [guests] in the synagogue [and lodged them there].
>
> C. R. Immi instructed the scribes, "If someone comes to you with some slight contact with Torah learning, receive him, his asses, and his belongings."
>
> D. R. Berekhiah went to the synagogue in Beisan. He saw someone rinsing his hands and feet in a fountain [in the courtyard of the synagogue]. He said to him, "It is forbidden to you [to do this]."
>
> E. The next day the man saw [Berekhiah] washing his hands and feet in the fountain.
>
> F. He said to him, "Rabbi, is it permitted to you and forbidden to me?"
>
> G. He said to him, "Yes."
>
> H. He said to him, "Why?"
>
> I. He said to him, "Because this is what R. Joshua b. Levi said, 'Synagogues and schoolhouses belong to sages and their disciples.'"

The extraordinary privileges accruing to sages' special status were material as well as symbolic. Sages in theory should not be paid for their learning. But they could accept a fee in compensation for the time they gave to teaching. In a setting in which people claimed lost property by having to describe what they had lost, sages were exempted from that requirement. Merely saying the property was theirs sufficed; they were assumed to be honest in all respects. Sages could indulge themselves by stretching the law to provide for their own ease and comfort. These three quite disparate elements point to the simple fact that the special standing of sages carried with it worldly benefits.

Y. Nedarim 4:3.II

    A. It is written, "Behold, I have taught you statutes and ordinances" [Deuteronomy 4:5].

    B. Just as I do so without pay, so you must do so without pay.

    C. Is it possible that the same rule applies to teaching Scripture and translation [cf. M. Nedarim 4:3D]?

    D. Scripture says, "Statutes and ordinances."

    E. Statutes and ordinances must you teach without pay, but you need not teach Scripture and translation without pay.

    F. And yet we see that those who teach Mishnah collect their pay.

    G. Said R. Judah b. R. Ishmael, "It is a fee for the use of their time [which they cannot utilize to earn a living for themselves] which they collect."

Y. Baba Mesia 2:8.III

    A. R. Judah said, "Disciples of sages do not have to indicate distinguishing characteristics."

Y. Besah 1:7.I

    K. R. Abbahu went down to bathe in the spring of Tiberias, and he would lean on two Goths as his guards. When they started to fall, he helped them up, and that happened twice. They said to him, "What's going on? [Why do you have to lean on us at all?]"

    L. He said to them, "I am saving my strength for my old age, [by leaning on you now]."

    M. R. Huna did not go down to the meetinghouse [on the festival day, wanting to save his strength, since he did not wish to walk].

    N. R. Qatina asked, "And has it not been taught: 'They may carry infirm folk'?"

It should not be supposed that we deal merely with the theory of how sages wished to conduct themselves and to be treated. Some stories indicate that, while meticulous about objectivity in decisions on property, sages were prepared in their courts to use their power to enforce their own demands for dignity and honor. Insulting or offending a sage therefore bore material, not merely spiritual, penalties, as in the following:

Y. Ketubot 4:7.IV

> A. R. Simeon b. Laqish in the name of R. Judah bar Haninah: "They voted in Usha in the case of him who insulted a sage [elder] and who hit him that one pays him compensation for the humiliation in toto [which is more than the compensation paid for damages to him]."
>
> B. There was a case of someone who insulted a sage and hit him, and he [was required to] pay him compensation for the humiliation in toto.

Y. Baba Qamma 8:6.I

> B. Someone taught in the name of R. Simeon b. Laqish, "He who humiliates a sage pays him the full compensation to be paid for his humiliation."
>
> C. Someone lost his temper with R. Judah b. Hanina. The case came before R. Simeon b. Laqish. He imposed on him a fine of a litra of gold.

We need hardly remind ourselves that sages prided themselves on the honesty and objectivity of their courts. They would not make use of their position for private gain. But they most certainly used their power to exact the high degree of respect they thought their due.

A socially sanctioned penalty imposed by sages involved ostracism or excommunication. Under these circumstances a sage could declare someone who had displeased him to be beyond the pale of the community. As the arbiter of society, the sage thus invoked a powerful penalty indeed. How a decree of ostracism worked in the setting of ordinary life, as distinct from the context of formal court action, is illustrated in the following.

Y. Moed Qatan 3:1.X

> G. A serving woman who worked for Bar Pata was passing by a synagogue, and she saw the teacher hit a

child more than was necessary. She said to him, "That man [you] should be in excommunication." He came and asked R. Aha [how to deal with what she had said]. He said to him, "You must take account of yourself [in the light of what she said]."

H. That is to say, He who does something which is improper is to be excommunicated.

I. R. Simeon b. Laqish was guarding figs in a garden. Thieves came and stole them by night. In the end he found out who they were. He said to them, "Let them be excommunicated." They said to him, "Let that man [you] be subject to a decree of excommunication."

J. He paid attention to what they had said. He said, "They owe me money, but did they owe me their life [that I put them into excommunication]? [Surely not. What I did was wrong.]"

K. He went and ran after them. He said to them, "Release me [from the decree of excommunication]."

L. They said to him, "Release us, and we shall release you."

M. That is to say, He who excommunicates him who should not be subject to excommunication—his act of excommunication still is valid.

The foregoing picture is how, in general, sages wished to see things. But the Talmud preserves a picture at sharp variance with the fantasy we have outlined. The following story tells us that, beyond the realm of disciples and sages, ordinary Israelites had their own view of matters and did not hesitate to carry out their wishes, even in the face of the sages' displeasure.

Y. Megillah 4:4.III

A. To R. Simeon, teacher of Trachonitis, the townspeople said, "Cut your reading short, so that our children may learn to read [by following it slowly]."

B. He came and asked R. Haninah. He said to him, "Even if they cut off your head, do not listen to them." So he did not listen to them, and they fired him from his job as teacher.

C. After a while he came down here [to Babylonia, where

the story was told]. R. Simon b. Yusinah dealt with him. He said to him, "What did you do in that town?" And he told him the story.

D. He said to him, "Why did you not listen to them, [and do what they wanted]?"

E. He said to him, "And do you do it that way?"

F. He said to him, "And do we not cut a verse into parts in the study session [so as to translate it bit by bit and learn it that way]?"

G. He said to him, "But do we not then go back and say the whole thing as one piece?"

H. Said R. Zeira, "If that teacher were alive in my time, I should appoint him as a sage."

Once more we conclude our review with evidence that the Talmud's rather lifeless picture of a society humbling itself to the sage is to be set alongside a quite separate and astringent fact that the sages were by no means the sole authorities in Jewry. The Big Men of the town controlled the town. The sages did not. Accordingly, when it came down to the wire, the local authorities could not be excommunicated, there being no social sanction effective against them. They fired the sage for not following their instructions, and he stayed fired. Accordingly, the rather ample account of the sages' special privileges is to be set in the balance against the Talmud's striking evidence of the tale-tellers' anxiety in the world beyond the pages of the text.

The clearest picture of the theory of the Torah contained within the Judaism to which the Talmud of the Land of Israel testifies is to be found in the sages' reading of Scripture. Specifically, the worldview projected by them upon the heroes of ancient Israel most clearly reveals the Talmud's sages' view of themselves and their world. The Talmud's framers naturally took for granted that the world they knew in the fourth century had flourished a thousand and more years earlier. The values they embodied and the supernatural powers they fantasized for themselves predictably were projected backward onto biblical figures. The ubiquitous citation of biblical proof-texts in support of both legal and technological statements shows the mentality of the Talmud's framers. In their imagination, everything they said stood in direct continuity with what Scripture had stated. Biblical and Talmudic authorities lived on a single plane of being, in a single age of shared discourse; the Mishnah and associated documents amply restated propositions held for all time and proved in Scripture too.

But it is inappropriate to dwell merely on the anachronistic reading of Scripture characteristic of Talmudic sages. That is a natural fact of the age. What is important is the theory of salvation thereby given its clearest statement. What was the rabbis' view of salvation? Seeing Scripture in their own model, they took the position that the Torah of old, its supernatural power and salvific promise, continued to endure—among themselves. In consequence, the promise of salvation contained in every line of Scripture was to be kept in every deed of learning and obedience to the law effected under their auspices. So while they projected backward the things they cherished in an act of (to us) extraordinary anachronism, in their eyes they carried forward, to their own time, the promise of salvation for Israel contained within the written Torah of old.

In this aspect the mode of thought and the consequent salvific proposition conformed to the model revealed likewise in the Gospel of Matthew. The reason Scripture was cited, for both statements on Israel's salvation, was not to establish authority alone, but to identify what was happening then with what had happened long ago. The purpose then was not merely to demonstrate and authenticate the bona fide character of a new figure of salvation, but to show the continuity of the salvific process. The point was that the figure at hand was not new at all. He stood as a renewed exemplar and avatar of Israel's eternal hope, now come to full realization—a very different thing. Authenticity hardly demanded demonstration of the Scriptural authority. That was the datum of the more extreme claim laid down in the profoundly anachronistic reading accorded to Scripture. In finding sages in the (written) Torah, therefore, the Talmud's sages implicitly stated a view of themselves as the continuation of the sanctified way of life of the written Torah. It followed that the pattern and promise of salvation contained therein lay within their way of life. That is the meaning of the explicit reading of the present into the past—the implicit arrogation of the hope of the past to the salvific heroes of the present: themselves.

To state matters simply, if David, King of Israel was like a rabbi today, then a rabbi today would be the figure of the son of David who was to come as King of Israel. It is not surprising, therefore, that among the many biblical heroes whom the Talmudic rabbis treated as sages, principal and foremost was David himself, now made into a messianic rabbi or a rabbinical Messiah. He was the sage of the Torah, the avatar and model for the sages of their own time. That view was made explicit, both specifically and in general terms. If a rabbi was jealous to have his traditions cited in his own name, it was because that was David's explicit view as well. In more general terms, both David and Moses are represented as students of Torah, just like the disciples and sages of the current time.

Y. Sanhedrin 2:6.IV

A. It is written, "And David said longingly, 'O that some-one would give me water to drink from the well of Bethlehem [which is by the gate]'" (I Chronicles 11:17).

B. R. Hiyya bar Ba said, "He required a teaching of law."

C. "Then the three mighty men broke through [the camp of the Philistines]" (I Chronicles 11:18).

D. Why three? Because the law is not decisively laid down by fewer than three.

E. "But David would not drink of it; [he poured it out to the Lord, and said, 'Far be it from me before my God that I should do this. Shall I drink the lifeblood of these men? For at the risk of their lives they brought it']" (I Chronicles 11:18-19).

F. David did not want the law to be laid down in his own name.

G. "He poured it out to the Lord"—establishing [the decision] as [an unattributed] teaching for the generations, [so that the law should be authoritative and so be cited anonymously].

Y. Sheqalim 2:4.V

O. David prayed for mercy for himself, as it is said, "Let me dwell in thy tent for ever! Oh to be safe under the shelter of thy wings, selah" (Psalm 61:4).

P. And did it enter David's mind that he would live for ever?

Q. But this is what David said before the Holy One, blessed be He, "Lord of the world, may I have the merit that my words will be stated in synagogues and schoolhouses."

R. Simeon b. Nazira in the name of R. Isaac said, "Every disciple in whose name people cite a teaching of law in this world—his lips murmur with him in the grave, as it is said, 'Your kisses are like the best wine that goes down smoothly, gliding over lips of those that sleep' (Song of Songs 7:9).

S. "Just as in the case of a mass of grapes, once a person puts his finger in it, forthwith even his lips begin to smack, so the lips of the righteous, when someone cites a teaching of the law in their names—their lips murmur with them in the grave."

Y. Berakhot 1:1.XII (translated by Tzvee Zahavy)

O. "I will awake the dawn" (Psalm 5:7, 8)—I will awaken the dawn; the dawn will not awaken me.

P. David's [evil] impulse tried to seduce him [to sin]. And it would say to him, "David. It is the custom of kings that awakens them. And you say, I will awake the dawn. It is the custom of kings that they sleep until the third hour [of the day]. And you say, At midnight I rise." And [David] used to say [in reply], "[I rise early] because of thy righteous ordinances" (Psalm 119:62).

Q. And what would David do? R. Phineas in the name of R. Eleazar b. R. Menahem [said], "He used to take a harp and lyre and set them at his bedside. And he would rise at midnight and play them so that the associates of Torah should hear. And what would the associates of Torah say? 'If David involves himself with Torah, how much more so should we.' We find that all of Israel was involved in Torah [study] on account of David."

Y. Horayot 3:5.I

E. R. Yohanan, "All these forty days that Moses served on the mountain, he studied the Torah but forgot it. In the end it was given to him as a gift. All this why? So as to bring the stupid students back to their studies [when they become discouraged]."

This long extract has shown us how the Talmud's authorities readily saw their concerns in biblical statements attributed to David. "Water" meant "a teaching of Torah." "Three mighty men" were of course judges.

At issue was whether or not the decision was to be stated in David's own name—and so removed from the authoritative consensus of sages. David exhibits precisely those concerns for the preservation of his views in his name that, in earlier sections, we saw attributed to rabbis. All of this, as we have noted, fully reveals the rabbis' deeper convictions when we remember that David, the rabbi, also was in everyone's mind David, the Messiah.

The projection of the present onto the past encompassed details as well as general propositions. One striking instance is that the quarrels of Israelite history were read as disputes remarkably like those of contemporary masters, for example, disputes about primacy in the order of precedence due to masters of Torah. Jeroboam's break with Rehoboam was interpreted in precisely this setting.

Y. Abodah Zarah 1:1.I

> RR. Said R. Yose bar Jacob, "It was at the conclusion of a sabbatical year that Jeroboam began to rule over Israel. That is the meaning of the following verse: '[And Moses commanded them.] At the end of every seven years, at the set time of the year of release, at the feast of booths, when all Israel comes to appear before the Lord your God at the place which He will choose, you shall read this law before all Israel in their hearing' (Deuteronomy 31:10-11).

> SS. "[Jeroboam] said, 'I shall be called upon to read [the Torah, as Scripture requires]. If I get up and read first, they will say to me, "The king of the place [in which the gathering takes place, namely, Jerusalem] comes first." And if I read second, it is disrespectful to me. And if I do not read at all, it is a humiliation for me. And, finally, if I let the people go up, they will abandon me and go over to the side of Rehoboam the son of Solomon.'"

The tale once again shows how contemporary conventions of courtesy owed to sages naturally applied, in the imaginations of the Talmud's framers, to the olden times. The parallels have already come before us.

That the rules governing relationships among sages or between masters and disciples were read into biblical times and relationships among biblical figures is illustrated in the following.

Y. Horayot 3:5.II

A. R. Joshua b. Levi said, "[If there] are a head [not a sage] and an elder [a sage], the elder takes precedence. For there is no head if there is no elder."

B. What is the scriptural evidence for this position?

C. "You stand this day all of you before the Lord your God; the heads of your tribes, your elders, and your officers, all the men of Israel" (Deuteronomy 29:10).

D. And it is written, "Then Joshua gathered all the tribes of Israel to Shechem, and summoned the elders, the heads, the judges, and the officers of Israel" (Joshua 24:1).

E. Thus Moses gave precedence to the heads over the elders, while Joshua gave precedence to the elders over the heads.

F. Moses, because all of them were his disciples, gave precedence to the heads over the elders. Joshua, because all of them were not his disciples, gave precedence to the elders [who were sages] over the heads [who were not sages].

G. Moses, because he did not yet have need of them for conquering the land, gave precedence to the heads over the elders. Joshua, because he needed them for conquering the land, gave precedence to the elders over the heads.

H. Moses, because he was not fatigued by the study of the Torah [having divine help], gave precedence to the heads over the elders. Joshua, because he was fatigued by study of the Torah, gave precedence to the elders over the heads.

I. R. Joshua of Sikhnin in the name of R. Levi: "Moses, because he foresaw through the Holy Spirit that the Israelites were destined to be imprisoned by the [gentile] kingdoms, and their heads would be standing over them [to deal with the Gentiles], gave precedence to the heads over the elders."

What is striking here is the glimpse we gain into the imagination of the Talmud's voice. It is also the certainty that reasons for contemporary organization of the rabbinical estate derived from the founding of Israel's

political institutions. This is explicit at H. I. then offers a different
approach to the matter, reflecting the issue of who dealt with the
Gentiles, and who did not. The elders were sages of Torah, the heads were
not. So the point in the end is not much different.

The institutions imagined by the framers of the Mishnah, chief
among them a Sanhedrin, ruling on disputed matters of law, were naturally envisioned in times past. The master–disciple circles of the day had
their counterpart in ancient Israel. Saul supported members of the
Sanhedrin, and King Hezekiah was subject to sages' opinions.

Y. Nedarim 9:9.I

    A. It is written, "Ye daughters of Israel, weep over Saul,
who clothed you daintily in scarlet, who put ornaments of gold upon your apparel" (2 Samuel 1:24).

    B. As to the views of R. Judah and R. Nehemiah, one of
them said, "The reference is actually to the daughters
of Israel, for when their husbands would go to war,
[Saul] would provide them with food.

    C. "Why does Scripture say, 'Who put ornaments of gold
upon your apparel'?

    D. "The meaning is that an ornament is beautiful only on
a lovely body."

    E. And the other said, "The reference is not to the daugh-
ters of Israel but to the builders of Israel, the Israelite
Sanhedrin. For Saul would spy out of a group of
associates and give them food and drink.

    F. "And what is the meaning of the statement of Scrip-
ture, 'Who put ornaments of gold upon your apparel'?

    G. "For he would listen to the reasoning for a law from a
sage and would praise him for it."

Y. Nedarim 6:1.III

    W. Six things did Hezekiah, the king of Judah, do. In
three of them [sages] agreed with him, and in three of
them they did not agree with him.

    X. He dragged his father's bones on a rope bier, he pul-
verized the brazen serpent, and he hid away the note-
book of remedies, and they agreed with him.

    Y. And in three things they did not agree with him: He

closed off the waters of Upper Gihon, he cut [the gold off] the doors of the Temple, and he intercalated the month of Nisan in Nisan itself [calling Nisan the second Adar after Nisan had already begun], and they did not agree with what he had done.

Not only did the Talmud's sages take for granted that the imaginary institutions of their own system, if not fully realized in their own time, surely functioned in olden times, but, more strikingly still, they also knew as fact that precisely the ways in which they reasoned about the law characterized the minds of their ancestors. Accordingly, their characteristic modes of thought simply carried forward those established in ancient Israel, deriving from God's revelation to Moses at Sinai. The dispute of Korah and Moses was a dispute not only about the law, but also about how to reason within the law.

Y. Sanhedrin 10:1.VII

I. Rab said, "Korah was an Epicurean. What did he do? He went and made a prayer shawl which was entirely purple [although the law is that only the fringe was to be purple]."

J. He went to Moses, saying to him, "Moses, our rabbi: A prayer shawl which is entirely purple, what is the law as to its being liable to show fringes?"

K. He said to him, "It is liable, for it is written, 'You shall make yourself tassles [on the four corners of your cloak with which you cover yourself]'" (Deuteronomy 22:12).

L. [Korah continued,] "A house which is entirely filled with holy books, what is the law as to its being liable for a mezuzah [containing sacred scripture, on the doorpost]?"

M. He said to him, "It is liable for a mezuzah, for it is written, 'And you shall write them on the doorposts of your house [and upon your gates]' (Deuteronomy 6:9)."

N. He said to him, "A bright spot the size of a bean— what is the law [as to whether it is a sign of uncleanness in line with Leviticus 13:2ff.]?"

O. He said to him, "It is a sign of uncleanness."

P. "And if it spread over the whole of the man's body?"

Q. He said to him, "It is a sign of cleanness."

R. At that moment Korah said, "The Torah does not come from Heaven, Moses is no prophet, and Aaron is not a high priest."

S. Then did Moses say, "Lord of all worlds, if from creation the earth was formed with a mouth, well and good, and if not, then make it now!"

This colloquy represents Moses and Korah as disputing about the requirements of Scriptural law and interpretation, just as any set of rabbis might do in the third and fourth centuries. Korah led Moses into a series of absurd positions, leading to the conclusion specified at R. Accordingly, a single mode of thought and analysis joined Israel's sages from Moses onward—and reaching false conclusions could be punished again as it was in the day of Korah.

For all their veneration of Scripture and its (rabbinical) heroes, the Talmud's authorities still regarded knowledge of the Mishnah as more important than knowledge of Scripture, citing biblical proof-texts in support of that proposition. The relative value of learning in various collections of Torah teachings is worked out in the following extended unit of discourse.

Y. Horayot 3:5.III

D. This is what has been said: The Mishnah takes precedence over Scripture.

E. And the following supports this tradition:

F. For R. Simeon b. Yohai taught, "He who takes up studies in Scripture—it is a good quality that is no good quality."

G. Rabbis treat Scripture as equivalent to the Mishnah . . .

W. R. Aha interpreted the following verse: "'A just balance and scales are the Lord's; all the weights in the bag are his work' (Proverbs 16:110).

X. "'A balance'—this refers to Scripture.

Y. "'Scales' refers to the Mishnah.

Z. "'Just' refers to the Talmud.

AA. "'Are the Lord's' refers to the Supplement [Tosefta].

BB. "'All the weights in the bag are his work'—all of them take their reward from one bag."

CC. R. Abba bar Kahana went to a certain place. He found R. Levi sitting and interpreting the following verse: "'A man to whom God gives wealth, possession, and honor, so that he lacks nothing of all that he desires, yet God does not give him power to enjoy them, but a stranger enjoys them' (Kohelet 6:2).

DD. "'Wealth'—this refers to Scripture.

EE. "'Possessions'—these are the laws.

FF. "'Honor'—this is the Supplement."

Christians as well as Jews, ordinary folk as well as sages, knew Scripture. So striking is one point not to be missed in the statement at hand. Given that Torah is the source of supernatural power and salvation, which part of Torah is the source of supernatural power and salvation and which part of Torah is to enjoy precedence? It quite obviously will be the Mishnah and its associated bodies of discussion, that is, the component of Torah in the hands of Israel and Israel's sages, alone. Assigning precedence to knowledge of Mishnah over knowledge of Scripture therefore serves to declare that those who master Mishnah possess a power to attain salvation greater than those who know (merely) Scripture. That I take to be the deeper sense of D-F.

The contrary view, G, W-BB, should not be missed. Both parties of course must be right. No one could really maintain that knowledge of the Scripture was secondary to knowledge of the Mishnah. Nor would any sage concur that knowledge of Scripture alone sufficed. So the sense of the passage allows for two correct, if distinct, positions to be juxtaposed. For our purpose the fundamental assertion of the identity of Scripture learning and Mishnah learning with "Torah" is the main thing. That commonplace suffices here, as everywhere else in our Talmud, to state that for which the Talmud's clerks and bureaucrats labored: attaining through learning in and embodiment of the Torah the salvation of Israel, now and at the end of days.

4

The Yerushalmi's Account
of History

To understand how the Yerushalmi develops a conception of history, we have to begin with the Mishnah's theory of the same matter. Only in this context shall we understand the full weight and meaning of the Yerushalmi's authorship's rethinking of the basic categories of events and their meaning. To begin with, the framers of the Mishnah present us with a kind of historical thinking quite different from the one that they, along with all Israel, had inherited in Scripture. The legacy of prophecy, apocalypse, and mythic-history (*Heilsgeschichte*) handed on by the writers of the books of the Old Testament exhibits a single and quite familiar conception of history seen whole. Events bear meaning, God's message, and judgment. What happens is singular, therefore, an event to be noted, and points toward lessons to be drawn for where things are heading and why. If things do not happen at random, they also do not form indifferent patterns of merely secular, social facts. What happens is important because of the meaning contained therein. That meaning is to be discovered and revealed through the narrative of what has happened. So for all forms of Judaism until the Mishnah, the writing of history serves as a form of prophecy. Just as prophecy takes up the interpretation of historical events, so historians retell these events in the frame of prophetic theses. And out of the two—historiography as a mode of mythic reflection, prophecy as a means of mythic construction—emerges a picture of future history. That picture, framed in terms of visions and supernatural symbols, in the end focuses, as much as do prophecy and history-writing, upon the here and now.

The upshot is simple. History consists of a sequence of one-time events, each singular, all meaningful. These events move from a beginning to an end at a foreordained goal. History moves toward eschatology, the end of history. The teleology of Israel's life finds its definition in eschatological fulfillment. Eschatology therefore constitutes not a choice within teleology, but the definition of teleology. History done in this way then sits enthroned as the queen of theological science. Events do not conform to patterns, they form patterns. What happens matters because events bear meaning, constitute history. Now, as is clear, such a conception of mythic and apocalyptic history comes to realization in the writing of history in the prophetic pattern or in the apocalyptic framework, both of them mythic modes of organizing events. We have every right to expect such a view of matters to lead people to write books of a certain type. In the case of Judaism, obviously, we should expect people to write history books that teach lessons or apocalyptic books that through pregnant imagery predict the future and record the direction and end of time. And in antiquity that kind of writing proves commonplace among all kinds of groups and characteristic of all sorts of Judaisms but one.

The Mishnah contains no sustained narrative whatsoever, a very few tales, and no large-scale conception of history. It organizes its system in nonhistorical and socially unspecific terms, lacking all precedent in prior systems of Judaism or in prior kinds of Judaic literature. Instead of narrative, it gives description of how things are done, that is, descriptive laws. Instead of reflection on the meaning and end of history, it constructs a world in which history plays little part. Instead of narratives full of didactic meaning, it provides lists of events so as to expose the traits that they share and thus the rules to which they conform. The definitive components of a historical-eschatological system of Judaism— description of events as one-time happenings, analysis of the meaning and end of events, and interpretation of the end and future of singular events—none of these constituents of all other systems of Judaism (including nascent Christianity) of ancient times finds a place in the Mishnah's system of Judaism.

So the Mishnah finds no precedent in prior Israelite writings for its mode of dealing with things that happen. The Mishnah's way of identifying happenings as consequential and describing them, its way of analyzing those events it chooses as bearing meaning, its interpretation of the future to which significant events point—all those in context were unique. Yet to say that the Mishnah's system is ahistorical could not be more wrong. The Mishnah presents a different kind of history. More to the point, it revises the inherited conception of history and reshapes that conception to fit into its own system. When we consider the power of the biblical myth, the force of its eschatological and messianic interpretation of history, the effect of apocalypse, we must find astonishing the capacity of the Mishnah's framers to think in a different way about the same things. A teleology constructed outside the eschatological mode of thought in the setting of the biblical world of ancient Israel proves amazing. Let me now show some of the principal texts that contain and convey this other conception of how events become history and how history teaches lessons.

By "history," as the opening discussion makes clear, I mean not merely events, but how events are so organized and narrated as to teach (for them, theological, for us, religious-historical or social) lessons, reveal patterns, tell us what we must do and why, what will happen to us tomorrow. In that context, some events contain richer lessons than others; the destruction of the Temple of Jerusalem teaches more than a crop failure, being kidnapped into slavery more than stubbing one's toe. Furthermore, lessons taught by events—"history" in the didactic sense—follow a progression from trivial and private to consequential and public. The framers of the Mishnah explicitly refer to very few events, treating those they do mention within a focus quite separate from what happened—the unfolding of the events themselves. They rarely create or use narratives. More probative still, historical events do not supply organizing categories or taxonomic classifications. We find no tractate devoted to the destruction of the Temple, no complete chapter detailing the events of Bar Kokhba, nor even a sustained celebration of the events of the sages' own historical life. When things that have happened are mentioned, it is neither in order to narrate, nor to interpret and draw lessons from, the event. It is either to illustrate a point of law or to pose a problem of the law—always en passant, never in a pointed way. So when sages refer to what has happened, it is casual and tangential to the main thrust of discourse. Famous events, of enduring meaning, such as the return to Zion from Babylonia in the time of Ezra and Nehemiah, gain entry into the Mishnah's discourse only because of the genealogical divisions of Israelite society into castes among the immigrants (M. Qiddushin 4:1). Where the Mishnah provides few tales or narratives, moreover, they more often treat how things in the cult are done in general than what, in particular, happened on any one day.[1] It is suffi-

---

[1] For instance, there is the tale of the burning of the red cow (M. Parah 3) or of the purification of the *mesora* of Leviticus 13:2ff. (M. Negaim 14). The names of Temple officers are catalogued (M. Sheqalim 51:1). But we learn no more about them than the jobs to which they were assigned. Allusions to famous events even within sages' own circles do not demand detailed narration (as to M. Kelim 5:10).

cient to refer casually to well-known incidents. Narrative, in the Mishnah's limited rhetorical repertoire, is reserved for the narrow framework
of what priests and others do on recurrent occasions and around the
Temple. In all, stories about dramatic events and important deeds, that
staple of history, provide little nourishment for the minds of the Mishnah's jurisprudents. Events, if they appear at all, are treated as trivial.
They may be well known, but are consequential in some way other than
is revealed in the detailed account of what actually happened.

Sages' treatment of events determines what in the Mishnah is important about what happens. Since the greatest event in the century and
a half, from c. 50 to c. 200 C.E., during which the Mishnah's materials came
into being, was the destruction of the Temple in 70 C.E., we must expect
the Mishnah's treatment of that incident to illustrate the document's
larger theory of history: what is important and unimportant about what
happens. The treatment of the destruction occurs in two ways. First, the
destruction of the Temple constitutes a noteworthy fact in the history of
the law. Why? Because various laws about rite and cult had to undergo
revision on account of the destruction. The following provides a stunningly apt example of how the Mishnah's philosophers regard what
actually happened as being simply changes in the law:

M. Rosh Hashanah 4:1-4

4:1   A. On the festival day of the New Year which coincided
        with the Sabbath—
        B. in the Temple they would sound the shofar.
        C. But not in the provinces.
        D. When the Temple was destroyed, Rabban Yohanan
        ben Zakkai made the rule that they should sound the
        shofar in every locale in which there was a court.
        E. Said R. Eleazar, "Rabban Yohanan b. Zakkai made
        that rule in the case of Jamnia alone."
        F. They said to him, "All the same are Jamnia and every
        locale in which there is a court."

4:2   A. And in this regard also was Jerusalem ahead of Jamnia:
        B. in every town which is within sight and sound [of
        Jerusalem], and nearby and able to come to Jerusa-
        lem, they sound the shofar.
        C. But as to Jamnia, they sound the shofar only in the
        court alone.

4:3   A. In olden times the lulab was taken up in the Temple for seven days, and in the provinces for one day.

B. When the Temple was destroyed, Rabban Yohanan ben Zakkai made the rule that in the provinces the lulab should be taken up for seven days, as a memorial to the Temple;

C. and that the day [the sixteenth of Nisan] on which the omer is waved should be wholly prohibited [in regard to the eating of new produce] (Mishnah Sukkah 3:12).

4:4   A. At first they would receive testimony about the new moon all day long.

B. One time the witnesses came late, and the Levites consequently were mixed up as to [what] song [they should sing].

C. They made the rule that they should receive testimony [about the new moon] only up to the afternoon offering.

D. Then, if witnesses came after the afternoon offering, they would treat that entire day as holy, and the next day as holy, too.

E. When the Temple was destroyed, Rabban Yohanan b. Zakkai made the rule that they should [once more] receive testimony about the new moon all day long.

F. Said R. Joshua b. Qorha, "This rule too did Rabban Yohanan B. Zakkai make:

G. "Even if the head of the court is located somewhere else, the witnesses should come only to the location of the council [to give testimony, and not to the location of the head of the court]."

The passages before us leave no doubt about what sages selected as important about the destruction: it produced changes in synagogue rites.

Second, although the sages surely mourned the destruction and the loss of Israel's principal mode of worship, and certainly recorded the event of the ninth of Ab in the year 70 c.e., they did so in their characteristic way: they listed the event as an item in a catalogue of things that are like one another and so demand the same response. But then the destruction no longer appears as a unique event. It is absorbed into a pattern of like disasters, all exhibiting similar taxonomic traits, events to which the

people, now well-schooled in tragedy, know full well the appropriate
response. So it is in demonstrating regularity that sages reveal their way
of coping. Then the uniqueness of the event fades away, and its mundane
character is emphasized. The power of taxonomy in imposing order upon
chaos once more does its healing work. The consequence was reassurance
that historical events obeyed discoverable laws. Israel's ongoing life
would override disruptive, one-time happenings. So catalogues of events,
as much as lists of species of melons, served as brilliant apologetic by
providing reassurance that nothing lies beyond the range and power of
ordering system and stabilizing pattern.

M. Taanit 4:6-7

4:6   A. Five events took place for our fathers on the seven-
              teenth of Tammuz, and five on the ninth of Ab.
           B. On the seventeenth of Tammuz (1) the tablets [of the
              Torah] were broken, (2) the daily whole offering was
              cancelled, (3) the city wall was breached, (4) Aposte-
              mos burned the Torah, and (5) he set up an idol in the
              Temple.
           C. On the ninth of Ab (1) the decree was made against
              our forefathers that they should not enter the land, (2)
              the first Temple and (3) the second [Temple] were
              destroyed, (4) Betar was taken, and (5) the city was
              ploughed up [after the war of Hadrian].
           D. When Ab comes, rejoicing diminishes.

4:7   A. In the week in which the ninth of Ab occurs it is
              prohibited to get a haircut and wash one's clothes.
           B. But on Thursday of that week these are permitted,
           C. because of the honor due to the Sabbath.
           D. On the eve of the ninth of Ab a person should not eat
              two prepared dishes, nor should one eat meat or drink
              wine.
           E. Rabban Simeon b. Gamaliel says, "He should make
              some change from ordinary procedures."
           F. R. Judah declares people obligated to turn over beds.
           G. But sages did not concur with him.

I include M. Taanit 4:7 to show the context in which the list of
M. Taanit 4:6 stands. The stunning calamities catalogued at M. Taanit 4:6

form groups, reveal common traits, so are subject to classification. Then
the laws of M. Taanit 4:7 provide regular rules for responding to, coping
with, these untimely catastrophes, all (fortuitously) in a single classification. So the raw materials of history are absorbed into the ahistorical,
supernatural system of the Mishnah. The process of absorption and
regularization of the unique and one-time moment is illustrated in the
passage at hand.

Along these same lines, the entire history of the cult, so critical in
the larger system created by the Mishnah's lawyers, produced a patterned, therefore sensible and intelligible, picture. As is clear, everything
that happened turned out to be susceptible to classification, once the
taxonomic traits were specified. A monothetic exercise, sorting out periods and their characteristics, took the place of narrative, to explain
things in its own way: first this, and then that, and, in consequence, the
other. So in the neutral turf of holy ground, as much as in the trembling
earth of the Temple mount, everything was absorbed into one thing, all
classified in its proper place and by its appropriate rule. Indeed, so far as
the lawyers proposed to write history at all, they wrote it into their
picture of the long tale of the way in which Israel served God: the places
in which the sacrificial labor was carried on, the people who did it, the
places in which the priests ate the meat left over for their portion after
God's portion was set aside and burned up. This "historical" account
forthwith generated precisely that problem of locating the regular and
orderly, which the philosophers loved to investigate: the intersection of
conflicting but equally correct taxonomic rules, as we see at M. Zebahim
14:9, below. The passage that follows therefore is history, so far as the
Mishnah's creators proposed to write history: the reduction of events to
rules forming compositions of regularity, therefore meaning:

M. Zebahim 14:4-9

14:4 I. A. Before the tabernacle was set up, (1) the high places
were permitted, and (2) [the sacrificial] service [was
done by] the first born [Numbers 3:12-13, 8:16-18].

B. When the tabernacle was set up, (1) the high places
were prohibited, and (2) the [sacrificial] service [was
done by] priests.

C. Most Holy Things were eaten within the veils, Lesser
Holy Things [were eaten] throughout the camp of
Israel.

14:5 II. A. They came to Gilgal.
B. The High places were permitted.
C. Most Holy Things were eaten within the veils, Lesser Holy things, anywhere.

14:6 III. A. They came to Shiloh.
B. The high places were prohibited.
C. (1) There was no roof-beam there, but below was a house of stone, and hangings above it, and (2) it was "the resting place" [Deuteronomy 12:0].
D. Most Holy Things were eaten within the veils, Lesser Holy Things and second-tithe [were eaten] in any place within sight [of Shiloh].

14:7 IV. A. They came to Nob and Gibeon.
B. The high places were permitted.
C. Most Holy Things were eaten within the veils, Lesser Holy Things, in all the towns of Israel.

14:8 V. A. They came to Jerusalem.
B. The high places were prohibited.
C. And they never again were permitted.
D. And it was "the inheritance" [Deuteronomy 12:9].
E. Most Holy things were eaten within the veils, Lesser Holy Things and second-tithe within the wall.

14:9 A. All the Holy things which one sanctified at the time of the prohibition of the high places and offered at the time of the prohibition of the high places outside—
B. lo, these are subject to the transgression of a positive commandment and a negative commandment, and they are liable on their account to extirpation [for sacrificing outside the designated place, Leviticus 17:8-9, M. Zebahim 13:1A].
C. [If] one sanctified them at the time of the permission of high places and offered them up at the time of the prohibition of high places,
D. lo, these are subject to transgression of a positive commandment and to a negative commandment, but they are not liable on their account to extirpation [since if the offerings had been sacrificed when they were sanctified, there should have been no violation].
E. [If] one sanctified them at the time of prohibition of

high places and offered them up at the time of the
permission of high places,

F. lo, these are subject to transgression of a positive
commandment, but they are not subject to a negative
commandment at all.

The authorship at hand had the option of narrative, but chose the
way of philosophy: generalization through classification, comparison, and
contrast. The inclusion of M. Zebahim 14:9, structurally matching
M. Taanit 4:7, shows us the goal of the historical composition. It is to set
forth rules that intersect and produce confusion, so that we may sort out
confusion and make sense of all the data. The upshot may now be stated
briefly.

The Mishnah absorbs into its encompassing system all events, small
and large. With what happens the sages accomplish what they do with
everything else: a vast labor of taxonomy, an immense construction of the
order and rules governing the classification of everything on earth and in
Heaven. The disruptive character of history—one-time events of ineluctable significance—scarcely impresses the philosophers. They find no
difficulty in showing that what appears unique and beyond classification
has in fact happened before and so falls within the range of trustworthy
rules and known procedures. Once history's components, one-time
events, lose their distinctiveness, then history as a didactic intellectual
construct, as a source of lessons and rules, also loses all pertinence. So
lessons and rules come from sorting things out and classifying them,
that is, from the procedures and modes of thought of the philosopher
seeking regularity. To this labor of taxonomy, the historian's way of
selecting data and arranging them into patterns of meaning to teach
lessons proves inconsequential. One-time events are not what matter.
The world is composed of nature and supernature. The repetitious laws
that count are those to be discovered in Heaven and, in Heaven's creation
and counterpart, earth. Keep those laws and things will work out. Break
them, and the result is predictable: calamity of whatever sort will super-
vene in accordance with the rules. But just because it is predictable, a
catastrophic happening testifies to what has always been and must
always be, in accordance with reliable rules and within categories already
discovered and well explained. That is why the lawyer-philosophers of
the mid-second century produced the Mishnah—to explain how things
are. Within the framework of well-classified rules, there could be messiahs, but no single Messiah (in Christian theological terms: *Geschichte*,
but no *Historie*).

Up to now I have contrasted "history" with "eternity," and framed matters in such a way that the Mishnah's system appears to have been ahistorical and antihistorical. Yet in fact the framers of the Mishnah recognized the past-ness of the past and hence, by definition, laid out a conception of the past that constitutes a historical doctrine. But it is a different conception from the familiar one. To express the difference, I point out that, for modern history-writing, what is important is to describe what is unique and individual, not what is ongoing and unremarkable. History is the story of change, development, and movement. For the thinkers of the Mishnah, historical patterning emerges as scientific knowledge does, through taxonomy, the classification of the unique and individual, the organization of change and movement within unchanging categories. That is why the dichotomy between history and eternity, change and permanence, signals an unnuanced exegesis of what was, in fact, a subtle and reflective doctrine of history. That doctrine proves entirely consistent with the large perspectives of scribes, from the ones who made omen-series in ancient Babylonia to the ones who made the Mishnah. That is why the category of salvation does not serve, but the one of sanctification fits admirably.

How, then, in the Mishnah as the foundation-document of Judaism, does history come to full conceptual expression? History as an account of a meaningful pattern of events, making sense of the past and giving guidance about the future, begins with the necessary conviction that events matter. The Mishnah's framers, however, present us with no elaborate theory of events, a fact fully consonant with their systematic points of insistence and encompassing concern. Events do not matter, one by one. The philosopher-lawyers exhibited no theory of history either. Their conception of Israel's destiny in no way called upon historical categories of either narrative or didactic explanation to describe and account for the future. The small importance attributed to the figure of the Messiah as an historical-eschatological figure, therefore, fully accords with the larger traits of the system as a whole. Let me say with emphasis: If what is important in Israel's existence is sanctification, an ongoing process, and not salvation, understood as a one-time event at the end, then no one will find reason to narrate history.

It provided an ample account and explanation of Israel's history and destiny. That story—Why us?—emerged as the generative problem of Judaism. So, to seek the map that shows the road from the Mishnah, at the beginning, to the fully articulated Judaism of the end of the formative age in late antiquity, we have to look elsewhere. For as to the path from the Mishnah through the Tosefta—this is not the way people went. And that brings us to the Yerushalmi's doctrine of history.

Disorderly historical events entered the system of the Mishnah and found their place within the larger framework of the Mishnah's orderly world. So to claim that the Mishnah's framers merely ignored what was happening would be incorrect. They worked out their own way of dealing with historical events, the disruptive power of which they not only conceded but freely recognized. Further, the Mishnah's authors did not intend to compose a history book or a work of prophecy or apocalypse. Even if they had wanted to narrate the course of events, they could hardly have done so through the medium of the Mishnah. Yet the Mishnah presents its philosophy in full awareness of the issues of historical calamity confronting the Jewish nation. So far as the philosophy of the document confronts the totality of Israel's existence, the Mishnah by definition also presents a philosophy of history.

The Mishnah's subordination of historical events contradicts the emphasis of a thousand years of Israelite thought. The biblical histories, the ancient prophets, the apocalyptic visionaries—all had testified that what happened mattered. Events carried the message of the living God. That is, events constituted history; they pointed toward, and so explained, Israel's destiny. An essentially ahistorical system of timeless sanctification, worked out through construction of an eternal rhythm centered on the movement of the moon and stars and seasons, represented a choice taken by few outside of the priesthood. For Israel had suffered enormous loss of life. As we shall see, the Yerushalmi of the Land of Israel takes these events seriously and treats them as unique and remarkable. The memories proved real. The hopes evoked by the Mishnah's promise of sanctification of the world in static perfection did not. For they had to compete with the grief of an entire century of mourning:

Y. Taanit 4:5

> X. B. Rabbi would derive by exegesis twenty-four tragic events from the verse: "The Lord has destroyed without mercy all the habitation of Jacob; in his wrath he has broken down the strongholds of the daughter of Judah; he has brought down to the ground in dishonor the kingdom and its rulers" (Lamentations 2:2).
>
> C. R. Yohanan derived sixty from the same verse.

D. Did R. Yohanan then find more than did Rabbi in the same verse?

E. But because Rabbi lived nearer to the destruction of the Temple, there were in the audience old men who remembered what had happened, and when he gave his exegesis, they would weep and fall silent and get up and leave.

We do not know whether things happened as the storyteller says. But the fact remains that the framers of the Yerushalmi preserved the observation that, in Rabbi's time, memories of world-shaking events continued to shape Israel's mind and imagination. For people like those portrayed here, the Mishnah's taxonomic classification of tragedy to accord with trustworthy rules cannot have solved many problems.

Accordingly, we should not be surprised to observe that the Yerushalmi of the Land of Israel contains evidence pointing toward substantial steps taken in rabbinical circles, away from the position of the Mishnah. We find materials that fall entirely outside the framework of historical doctrine established within the Mishnah. These are, first, an interest in the periodization of history, and second, a willingness to include events of far greater diversity than those in the Mishnah. So the Yerushalmi contains an expanded view of the range of human life encompassed to begin with by the conception of history.

Let us take the second point first. So far as things happen that demand attention and so constitute "events," within the Mishnah these fall into two classifications: (1) biblical history, and (2) events involving the Temple. A glance at the catalogue, cited above from M. Taanit 4:6, tells us what kind of happening constitutes an "event," a historical datum demanding attention and interpretation. In the Yerushalmi at hand, by contrast, in addition to Temple-events, we find also two other sorts of *Geschichten*: Torah-events, that is, important stories about the legal and supernatural doings of rabbis, and also political events.

These events, moreover, involved people not considered in the Mishnah: Gentiles as much as Jews, Rome as much as Israel. The Mishnah's history, such as it is, knows only Israel. The Yerushalmi greatly expands the range of historical interest when it develops a theory of Rome's relationship to Israel and, of necessity also, Israel's relationship to Rome.

Only by taking account of the world at large can the Yerushalmi's theory of history yield a philosophy of history worthy of the name, that is, an account of who Israel is, the meaning of what happens to Israel, and the destiny of Israel in this world and at the end of time. Israel by itself—as the priests had claimed—lived in eternity, beyond time. Israel and Rome together struggled in historical time: an age with a beginning, a middle, and an end. That is the importance of the expanded range of historical topics found in the present Yerushalmi. When, in the other Talmud, created in Babylonia, we find a still broader interest, in Iran as much as Rome, in the sequence of world empires past and present, we see how rich and encompassing a theory of historical events begins with a simple step toward a universal perspective. It was a step that I think, unlike the ancient prophets and apocalyptists, the scribes and priests of the Mishnah were incapable of taking.

The concept of periodization—the raw material of historical thought—hardly presents surprises, since apocalyptic writers began their work by differentiating one age from another. When the Mishnah includes a statement of the "periods" into which time is divided, however, it speaks only of stages of the cult: Shiloh, Nob, Jerusalem. One age is differentiated from the next not by reference to historical changes but only by the location of sacrifice and the eating of the victim. The rules governing each locale impose taxa upon otherwise undifferentiated time. So periodization constitutes a function of the larger system of sanctification through sacrifice. The contrast between "this world" and "the world to come," which is not a narrowly historical conception in the Mishnah, now finds a counterpart in the Yerushalmi's contrast between "this age" and the age in which the Temple stood. And that distinction is very much an act of worldly historical differentiation. It yields not only apocalyptic speculation, but also generates sober and worldly reflection on the movement of events and the meaning of history in the prophetic–apocalyptic tradition. Accordingly, the Yerushalmi of the Land of Israel presents both the expected amplification of the established concepts familiar from the Mishnah, and also a separate set of ideas, perhaps rooted in prior times but still autonomous of what the Mishnah in particular had encompassed.

Let us first survey what is new and striking. From the viewpoint of the Mishnah, as I have suggested, the single most unlikely development is interest in the history of a nation other than Israel. For the Mishnah views the world beyond the sacred Land as unclean, tainted in particular with corpse-uncleanness. Outside the holy lies the realm of death. The faces of that world are painted in the monotonous white of the grave. Only within the range of the sacred do things happen. There, events may be classified and arranged, all in relationship to the Temple and its cult. But, standing majestically unchanged by the vicissitudes of time, the cult rises above history. Now the ancient Israelite interest in the history of the great empires of the world—perceived, to be sure, in relationship to the history of Israel—reemerges within the framework of the documents that succeeded the Mishnah. Naturally, in the Land of Israel only one empire mattered. This is Rome, which, in the Yerushalmi, is viewed solely as the counterpart to Israel. The world then consists of two nations: Israel, the weaker, Rome, the stronger. (This view varies somewhat from that of Leviticus Rabbah, seen in Chapter One.) Jews enjoy a sense of vastly enhanced importance when they contemplate such a world, containing as it does only two peoples that matter, one of whom is Israel. But from our perspective, the utility for the morale of the defeated people holds no interest. What strikes us is the evidence of the formation of a second and separate system of historical interpretation, beyond that of the Mishnah.

History and doctrine merge, with history made to yield doctrine. What is stunning is the perception of Rome as an autonomous actor, that is, as an entity with a point of origin, just as Israel has a point of origin, and a tradition of wisdom, just as Israel has such a tradition. These are the two points at which the large-scale conception of historical Israel finds a counterpart in the present literary composition. This sense of poised opposites, Israel and Rome, comes to expression in two ways.

First, as we shall now see, it is Israel's own history that calls into being its counterpart, the antihistory of Rome. Without Israel, there would be no Rome—a wonderful consolation to the defeated nation. For if Israel's sin created Rome's power, then Israel's repentance will bring Rome's downfall. Here is the way in which the Yerushalmi presents the match:

Y. Abodah Zarah 1:2

> IV. E. Saturnalia means "hidden hatred" (sinaah temunah): The Lord hates, takes vengeance, and punishes.
>
> F. This is in accord with the following verse: "Now Esau hated Jacob" (Genesis 27:41).
>
> G. Said R. Isaac b. R. Eleazar, "In Rome they call it Esau's Saturnalia."
>
> H. Kratesis: It is the day on which the Romans seized power.
>
> I. Said R. Levi, "It is the day on which Solomon intermarried with the family of Pharaoh Neccho, King of Egypt. On that day Michael came down and thrust a reed into the sea, and pulled up muddy alluvium, and

this was turned into a huge pot, and this was the great city of Rome. On the day on which Jeroboam set up the two golden calves, Remus and Romulus came and built two huts in the city of Rome. On the day on which Elijah disappeared, a king was appointed in Rome: "There was no king in Edom, a deputy was king" (1 Kings 22:47).

The important point is that Solomon's sin provoked Heaven's founding of Rome, thus history, lived by Israel, and provoking antihistory, lived by Rome.

Quite naturally, the conception of history and antihistory will assign to the actors in the antihistory—the Romans—motives explicable in terms of history, that is, the history of Israel. The entire world and what happens in it enter into the framework of meaning established by Israel's Torah. So what the Romans do, their historical actions, can be explained in terms of Israel's conception of the world. A striking example of the tendency to explain Romans' deeds through Israel's logic is the reason given for Trajan's war against the Jews:

Y. Sukkah 5:1

VII. A. In the time of Tronianus, the evil one, a son was born to him on the ninth of Ab, and the Israelites were fasting.

B. His daughter died on Hanukkah, and the Israelites lit candles.

C. His wife sent a message to him, saying, "Instead of going out to conquer the barbarians, come and conquer the Jews, who have rebelled against you."

D. He thought that the trip would take ten days, but he arrived in five.

E. He came and found the Israelites occupied in study of the Light of Torah, with the following verse: "The Lord will bring a nation against you from afar, from the end of the earth, as swift as the eagle flies, a nation whose language you do not understand" (Deuteronomy 28:49).

F. He said to them, "With what are you occupied?"

G. They said to him, "With thus-and-so."

    H. He said to them, "That man [I] thought that it would take ten days to make the trip, but arrived in five days." His legions surrounded them and killed them.

    I. He said to the women, "Obey my legions, and I shall not kill you."

    J. They said to him, "What you did to the ones who have fallen do also to us who are yet standing."

    K. He mingled their blood with the blood of their men, until the blood flowed into the ocean as far as Cyprus.

    L. At that moment the horn of Israel was cut off, and it is not destined to return to its place until the son of David will come.

What is important here is the source of what we might call "historical explanation," deriving, as it does, from the larger framework of sages' conviction. Trajan had done nothing except with God's help and by God's design. Here is another example:

Y. Gittin 5:7

    I. A. In the beginning the Romans decreed oppression against Judah, for they had a tradition in their hands from their forefathers that Judah had slain Esau, for it is written, "Your hand shall be on the neck of your enemies" (Genesis 49:8).

This means, again, that things make sense wholly in the categories of Torah. The world retains its logic, and Israel knows (and can manipulate) that logic.

At the foundations is the tension between Israel's God and pagan gods. That is, historical explanation here invokes the familiar polemic of Scripture. Accordingly, the development of an interest in Roman history—of a willingness to take as important, events in the history of some nation other than Israel—flows from an established (and rather wooden) notion of the world in which God and gods ("idols") compete. Israel's history of subjugation testifies, not to the weakness of Israel's God, but to His strength. The present prosperity of idolators, involving the subjugation of Israel, attests only to God's remarkable patience, God's love for the world He made. This conception, familiar to be sure in the Mishnah itself, now becomes absorbed into historical categories of "now" and "then." That is to say, the notion of competition between God and no-gods, Israel and Rome, is set within the framework of differentiation between (1) "this age" and (2) "the time to come." Since that notion marks a stop beyond the way in which the same theme had come to expression in Mishnah and Tosefta, we had best review the development of the same passage in its literary—hence canonical—sequences. The passage of the Mishnah is given in boldface type, of the Tosefta in italics. This helps us see the formation of the passage as a whole.

Y. Abodah Zarah 4:7

    A. They asked the sages in Rome, "If God is not in favor of idolatry why does he not wipe it out?"

    B. They said to them, "If people worshiped something of which the world had no need, he certainly would wipe it out."

    C. "But lo, people worship the sun, moon, stars, and planets.

    D. "Now do you think he is going to wipe out his world because of idiots?"

    E. They said to them, "If so, let them destroy something of which the world has no need, and leave something that the world needs!"

    F. They said to them, "Then we should strengthen the hands of those who worship these, which would not be destroyed, for then they would say, 'Now you know full well that they are gods, for lo, they were not wiped out!'"

I. A. Philosophers asked the sages in Rome, "If God is not in favor of idolatry, why does he not wipe it out?" They said to them, "If people worshiped something of which the world had no need, he certainly would wipe it out. But lo, people worship the sun, moon, and stars. Now do you think he is going to wipe out his world because of idiots?" [M. Abodah Zarah 4:7A-D]

    B. *"But let the world be in accord with its accustomed way, and the idiots who behave ruinously will ultimately come and give a full account of themselves. If one has stolen seeds for planting, are they not ultimately going to sprout? If one has had sexual relations with a married woman, will she not ultimately give birth? But let*

*the world follow its accustomed way, and the idiots who
behave ruinously will ultimately come and give a full
account of themselves" [Abodah Zarah 6:7]*

II. A. Said R. Zeira, "If it were written, 'Those who worship
them are like them,' there would be a problem. Are
those who worship the sun like the sun, those who
worship the moon like the moon?! But this is what is
written: 'Those who make them are like them; so are
all who trust in them' (Psalm 115:8)."

   B. Said R. Mana, "If it were written, 'Those who worship
them are like them,' it would pose no problem whatsoever. For it also is written, 'Then the moon will be
confounded, and the sun ashamed'" (Isaiah 24:23).

   C. R. Nahman in the name of R. Mana, "Idolatry is
destined in the end to come and spit in the face of
those that worship idols, and it will bring them to
shame and cause them to be nullified from the world."

   D. Now what is the scriptural basis for that statement?

   E. "All the worshipers of images will be put to shame,
who make their boast in worthless idols" (Psalm 97:7).

   F. R. Nahman in the name of R. Mana, "Idolatry is
destined in time to come to bow down before the Holy
One, blessed be He, and then be nullified from the
world."

   G. What is the scriptural basis for that statement?

   H. "All worshipers of images will be put to shame . . . : all
gods bow down before him" (Psalm 97:7).

The important point comes at II.C–H, at which the Yerushalmi's
sages present a temporal differentiation absent in the Mishnah. The
problem of the Mishnah is a philosophical one. The Tosefta's anonymous
authorities make that point explicit. There is a certain logic, an inevita-
bility, upon which Israel may rely. True, idolatry prospers. But idolators
will be called to account. Now that essentially attemporal notion, which
can sustain the interpretation of a last judgment for individuals, moves
into a social, hence temporal-historical, framework at the third stage. Not
merely the idolator, as an individual, comes to account but the age of
idolatry itself will come to an end. We differentiate between this age,
which is bad, and another age, a period in time, which will be good. The
notion of temporal sequences upon which historical thinking rests in no

way serves the framers of the Mishnah passage. By contrast, it is essential to the thought, concerning idolatry, of the authorities cited in the Yerushalmi.

The concept of two histories, balanced opposite one another, comes to particular expression, with the Yerushalmi, in the balance of Israelite sage and Roman emperor. Just as Israel and Rome, God and no-gods, compete, with a preordained conclusion, so do sage and emperor. In this age, it appears that the emperor has the power, as does Rome, as do the pagan gods with their temples in full glory. God's Temple, by contrast, lies in ruins. But just as sages overcome the emperor through their inherent supernatural power, so too will Israel and Israel's God in the coming age control the course of events.

Y. Terumot 8:10 (Translated by Alan J. Avery-Peck)

IV. A. As to Diocles the swineherd, the students of R. Yudan, the Patriarch, would make fun of him.

B. He [Diocletian] became emperor and moved to Paneas.

C. He sent letters to the rabbis, [saying]: "You must be here [to see] me immediately after the end of the [coming] Sabbath."

D. He instructed the messenger [who was to deliver these orders], "Do not give them the letters until the eve [of Sabbath], just as the sun is setting." [Diocletian hoped to force the rabbis to miss the appointment, for they would not travel on the Sabbath. Then he could have revenge on them because of their cavalier treatment of him, A.]

E. The messenger came to them on the eve [of Sabbath] as the sun was setting.

F. [After receiving the message] R. Yudan the Patriarch and R. Samuel bar Nahman were sitting in the public baths in Tiberias. Antigris, [a certain spirit, appeared and] came to their side.

G. R. Yudan, the Patriarch, wished to rebuke him [and chase him away].

H. R. Samuel bar Nahman said to him [Yudan], "Leave him be. He appears as a messenger of salvation."

I. [Antigris] said to them, "What is troubling the rabbis?"

J. They told him the story [and] he said to them, "[Finish] bathing [in honor of the Sabbath]. For your creator is going to perform miracles [for you]."

K. At the end of the Sabbath [Antigris] took them and placed them [in Paneas].

L. They told [the emperor], "Lo, the rabbis are outside!"

M. He said, "They shall not see my face until they have bathed."

N. [Diocletian] had the bath heated for seven days and nights, [so that the rabbis could not stand the heat].

O. [To make it possible for them to enter, Antigris] went in before them and overpowered the heat.

P. [Afterwards] they went and stood before [the king].

Q. He said to them, "Is it because your creator performs miracles for you that you despise the [Roman] Empire?"

R. They said to him, "Diocles the swineherd did we despise. But Diocletian the emperor we do not despise."

S. Diocletian said to them, "Even so, you should not rebuke [anyone], neither a young Roman, nor a young associate [of the rabbis, for you never know what greatness that individual will attain]."

The practical wisdom contained at the end should not blind us to the importance of the story within the larger theory of history presented in the Yerushalmi. The Mishnah finds ample place for debates between "philosophers" and rabbis. But in the Mishnah, the high priest in the Temple and the king upon his throne do not stand poised against, as equal and opposite powers, the pagan priest in his temple and the Roman emperor on his throne. The very conception is inconceivable within the context of the Mishnah. For the Yerushalmi, by contrast, two stunning innovations appear: first, the notion of emperor and sage in mortal struggle; second, the idea of an age of idolatry and an age beyond idolatry. The world had to move into a new orbit indeed for Rome to enter into the historical context formerly defined wholly by what happened to Israel.

To our secular eyes these developments seem perfectly natural. After all, the Jews really had been conquered. Their Temple really had been destroyed. So why should they not have taken an interest in the history of the conqueror and tried to place into relationship with their own history the things that happened to him? We find self-evident, moreover, the comfort to be derived from the explanations consequent upon the inclusion of Roman history in the Yerushalmi's doctrine of the world. But Israel had been defeated many times before the composition of the Mishnah, and the Temple had lain in ruins for nearly a century and a half when Judah the Patriarch promulgated the Mishnah as Israel's code of law. So the circumstances in which the Yerushalmi's materials were composed hardly differed materially from the condition in which, from Bar Kokhba onward, sages selected from what was available and composed the Mishnah.

The Scriptures, after all, also offered testimony to the centrality of history as a sequence of meaningful events. To the message and uses of history as a source of teleology for an Israelite system, biblical writings amply testified. Prophecy and apocalyptic had long coped quite well with defeat and dislocation. Yet, in the Mishnah, Israel's deeds found no counterpart in Roman history, while, in the Palestinian Yerushalmi, they did. In the Mishnah, time is differentiated entirely in other than national-historical categories. For, as in Abot, "this world" is when one is alive, "the world to come" is when a person dies. True, we find also "this world" and "the time of the Messiah." But detailed differentiation among the ages of "this world" or "this age" hardly generates problems in mishnaic thought. Indeed, no such differentiation appears. Accordingly, the developments briefly outlined up to this point constitute a significant shift in the course of intellectual events, to which the sources at hand— the Mishnah, Tosefta, and Yerushalmi of the Land of Israel—amply testify.

Differentiation between the time in which the Temple stood and the present age, of course, hardly will have surprised the authors of the Mishnah. It was a natural outcome of the Mishnah's own division of ages. We recall how time was divided by the location of the altar, and how the divisions were explained by reference to what was done in that regard. Now we find a specification of the exact years involved. Not surprisingly, however, since the Mishnah does not speculate on when the Temple will be rebuilt, as in Tosefta, so here, the framers of the passage in Yerushalmi do not specify the year in which they think the Temple will be rebuilt. The Messiah's coming plays no role at all.

Y. Megillah 1:12

> XI. O. So with the tent of meeting: it spent forty years less one in Gilgal. In Gilgal it spent fourteen years, seven when they were conquering the land and seven when they were dividing it.

P. In Shilo it spent three hundred and sixty-nine years.
Q. In Nob and Gibeon it spent fifty-seven years, thirteen
   in Nob and forty-four in Gibeon.
R. In Jerusalem in the time of the first building it was
   there for four hundred and ten years.
S. In the time of the second building it was four hundred
   ten years. This was meant to fulfill the statement of
   Scripture: "The latter splendor of this house shall be
   greater than the former, says the Lord of hosts; and in
   this place I will give prosperity, says the Lord of
   hosts" (Haggai 2:9).

Strikingly absent is any prediction as to when the third temple
would be rebuilt. In due course many would take up the work of speculation and calculation. But, in his exegesis of the Mishnah, the author of
this passage does not do so.

The principal point of differentiation between one age and another
now remained the destruction of the Temple, which, in the spirit of M.
Sotah 9:15, marked the turn of the age. Rules held applicable to Temple
times were reexamined to see whether they continued to apply. For
example, "What is the law as to tearing one's garments at this time upon
hearing God cursed in euphemisms?" (Y. Sanhedrin 7:8 VII.C). But the
important point is the least blatant. Not everything bad in the current
age was to be blamed on the destruction. The explanation of contention in
discussions of the law, for instance, involved not the differentiation
between historical periods, but the (timeless) failure of the disciples. "In
the beginning there was no contention; but ill-prepared disciples caused
it" (Y. Hagigah 2:IC). But the end of the matter still turns upon history:
"The Torah is not going to be restored to its wholeness until the son of
David comes (ibid., E). In context, the meaning is, "a long time from
now." The step seems a small one. "This age" and "the other age" shifted
at 70. Now, as soon as some other point of differentiation enters, not
based upon the destruction of the Temple, a new possibility emerges.
Specifically, the potentiality for a theory of Israel's life not spun out of
the cult and its history begins to move toward realization. That much we
can deduce from the slight evidence at hand.

A further mark of the development of interest in differentiating
among historical periods is found in the commemoration of important
events. Once one day is differentiated from another because of what
happened on that same date a long time ago, we move away from the
Mishnah's principal criterion for distinguishing the passage of time.

How so? The framers of the Mishnah, following the priestly tradition, knew that one day differs from another because of the passage of the moon through fixed stars in heaven (e.g., Passover falls at the first full moon after the vernal equinox) and the consequent revision of the cultic offerings on earth (as at Numbers 28-29). True, as we noticed, sages also absorbed into their system one-time historical events, such as the seventeenth of Tammuz and the ninth of Ab. But those events proved incidental to the construction of a larger system, with Mishnah's tractates named for festivals of the natural year and focused upon Temple rites for those days. When, therefore, we discover units of discourse devoted to specific historical events and their meaning, we find ourselves in a new situation. Why? Because events we regard as historical, as distinct from those we see as natural or supernatural, also have now come to be taken seriously. One day differs from another not by virtue of the criterion of creation, but on account of a political or other historical event. As we recognize, the only such historical, non-natural, event absorbed into the Mishnah's system involved the Temple. Accordingly, in what follows, we deal with a different approach to time from the one characteristic of the Mishnah's system.

Let me explain. Having evidently inherited from former times a calendar of celebrations of important events in Israel's history, marked by the prohibition against fasting, the Yerushalmi's sages pursued the issue. In the following unit of discourse we find attention to the traits of commemorative days, consonant with the interest in historical periodization noted earlier:

Y. Megillah 1:4

> IX. B. On the twelfth of that month [of Adar] is Tirion's day. [That day on which the decrees of Trajan were annulled is a holiday and it is forbidden to fast on that day, contrary to Meir's view of acceptable behavior on the twelfth of Adar, in line with M. Megillah 1:4G.]
>
> C. And R. Jacob bar Aha said, "Tirion's day has been annulled, for it is the day on which Lulianos and Pappos were killed."
>
> D. The thirteenth of that month of Adar is Nicanor's Day.
>
> E. What is Nicanor's Day? The ruler of the Kingdom of Greece was passing by the Land of Israel on route to Alexandria. He saw Jerusalem and broke out into cursing and execration, saying, "When I come back in

peace, I shall break down that tower." The members of
the Hasmonaean household went forth and did battle
with his troops and killed them until they came to see
those nearest the king. When they reached the troops
nearest the king, they cut off the hand of the king and
chopped off his head and stuck them on a pole, and
wrote underneath them, "Here is the mouth that
spoke shamefully and the hand that stretched out
arrogantly." These he set up on a pike in sight of
Jerusalem.

The importance of this passage is that attention focuses upon the
meaning of days distinguished because of specific, one-time events that
took place on them. There is no further taxonomic interest. The events
are of a clearly historical character—that is, in no way related to the cult
or the natural course of the moon in the heavens—and bear no claim that
what happens matters only if the Temple is directly affected. True, in the
background the Temple always is an issue. Further, the days under
discussion appear on the so-called Fasting Scroll, on which it is forbidden to mourn; hence all the events fell into a single taxon. Yet the
Mishnah's treatment of that matter neglects the very thing the Yerushalmi's authorities take up: the specifics of what happened, the exegesis,
in its own terms, of the Scroll and the events to which it refers. And that
is the main point. The framers of the passage at hand move out beyond
the limits of the Mishnah's system when they narrate events essentially
autonomous of happenings in the cult. Such events moreover are distinguished from one another and in no way forced into a uniform taxon. In
this step, as in others we have reviewed, we see how the authors represented in the Yerushalmi move into a framework of thought in which
Israel's being is described and interpreted in historical–eschatological
terms, not in natural–supernatural ones.

Still, the Temple's destruction would always mark the caesura of
time. Important political events were to be dated in relationship to that
date. Israel lost the right to judge capital cases "forty years before the
Temple was destroyed" (Y. Sanhedrin 7:2III.A). So, too, forty years
before the destruction, ominous signs of the coming end began to appear:

Y. Sotah 6:3

IV. A. Forty years before the destruction of the Temple the
western light went out, the crimson thread remained

crimson, and the lot for the Lord always came up in
the left hand.

B. They would close the gates of the Temple by night and
get up in the morning and find them wide open.

C. Said Rabban Yohanan ben Zakkai to the Temple, "O
Temple, why do you frighten us? We know that you
will end up destroyed.

D. "For it has been said, 'Open your doors, O Lebanon, that
the fire may devour your cedars!'" (Zechariah 11:1).

Reference to the destruction of the Temple as a principal landmark in
the division of history is hardly surprising. The framers of the Mishnah
surely will not have been surprised, since, for them, as M. Sotah 9:15 shows,
with the destruction, the old age had turned into the new and darkening
one. What was important to them was to find the counterpart in the life
of the sages, since the holy life of the Temple and the holy life of the
Torah-circles matched one another. So, in all, the Temple continued to provide the principal, and generative, paradigm—whether historical or cultic.

But as I have emphasized, the definition of significant, hence historical, events now expanded to encompass things that happened beyond the
Temple walls, yet still in connection with the Temple's destruction. The
main point is that, in the Yerushalmi at hand, the established symmetry
was shattered. The Temple's destruction had been made the counterpoise
to the decline in the generations of sages. But now the Temple's destruction stood for much more, testified, so to speak, in a wider variety of
cases, then solely to the decline of the supernatural world, whether
priestly or scribal (to use our terms, not theirs). The message of M. Sotah
9:15 was one thing, the message of the tales at hand, a larger and more
encompassing story. That, then, is the turning point, the transformation
of the Temple's destruction into an event bearing consequences in many
other ways.

The most important change is the shift in historical thinking adum-
brated in the pages of the Yerushalmi, a shift from focus upon the
Temple and its supernatural history to close attention to the people,
Israel, and its natural, this-worldly history. Once Israel, holy Israel, had
come to form the counterpart to the Temple and its supernatural life, that
other history—Israel's—would stand at the center of things. Accordingly, a new sort of memorable event came to the fore in the Yerushalmi
of the Land of Israel. Let me give this new history appropriate emphasis:
It was the story of the suffering of Israel, the remembrance of that
suffering, on the one side, and the effort to explain events of that tragic

kind, on the other. So a composite "history" constructed out of the Yerushalmi's units of discourse pertinent to consequential events would contain long chapters on what happened to Israel, the Jewish people, and not only, or mainly, what had earlier occurred in the Temple.

This expansion in the range of historical interest and theme forms the counterpart to the emphasis, throughout the law, upon the enduring sanctity of Israel, the people, that paralleled the sanctity of the Temple in its time. What is striking in the Yerushalmi's materials on Israel's suffering is the sages' interest in finding a motive for what the Romans had done. That motive derived specifically from the repertoire of explanations already available in Israelite thought. In adducing scriptural reasons for the Roman policy, as we saw, sages extended to the world at large that same principle of intelligibility, in terms of Israel's own Scripture and logic that, in the law itself, made everything sensible and reliable. So the labor of history-writing (or at least, telling stories about historical events) went together with the work of law-making. The whole formed a single exercise in explanation of things that had happened—that is, historical explanation. True, one enterprise involved historical events, the other legal constructions. But the outcome was one and the same.

The components of the historical theory of Israel's sufferings were manifold. First and foremost, history taught moral lessons. Historical events entered into the construction of a teleology for the Yerushalmi's system of Judaism as a whole. What the law demanded reflected the consequences of wrongful action on the part of Israel. So, again, Israel's own deeds defined the events of history. Rome's role, like Assyria's and Babylonia's, depended upon Israel's provoking divine wrath, executed by the great empire. This mode of thought comes to simple expression in what follows.

Y. Erubin 3:9

> IV. B. R. Ba, R. Hiyya in the name of R. Yohanan: "'Do not gaze at me because I am swarthy, because the sun has scorched me. My mother's sons were angry with me, they made me keeper of the vineyards; but, my own vineyard, I have not kept!' (Song of Songs 1:6). What made me guard the vineyards? It is because of not keeping my own vineyard.
>
> C. "What made me keep two festival days in Syria? It is because I did not keep the proper festival day in the Holy Land.

D. "'I imagined that I would receive a reward for the two days, but I receive a reward only for one of them.

E. "'Who made it necessary that I should have to separate two pieces of dough-offering from grain grown in Syria? It is because I did not separate a single piece of dough-offering in the Land of Israel.'"

Israel needed to learn the lesson of its history. When it did so, it also would take command of its own destiny. But this notion of framing one's own destiny should not be misunderstood. The framers of the Yerushalmi of the Land of Israel were not telling the Jews to please God by doing commandments in order that they should thereby gain control of their own destiny.

To the contrary, the paradox of the Yerushalmi's system lies in the fact that Israel frees itself of control by other nations only by humbly agreeing to accept God's rule instead. The nations—Rome, in the present instance—rest in one pan of the balance, while God rests, as it were, in the other. Israel must then choose between them. There is no such thing, for Israel, as freedom from both God and the nations, total autonomy and independence. There is only a choice of masters, a ruler on earth or a ruler in Heaven.

With propositions such as these, the framers of the Mishnah will assuredly have concurred. And why not? For the fundamental affirmations of the Mishnah about the centrality of Israel's perfection in stasis—sanctification—readily prove congruent to the attitudes at hand. Once the Messiah's coming had become conditional upon Israel's condition, not upon Israel's actions in historical time, then the Mishnah's system will have imposed its fundamental and definitive character upon the Messiah-myth. An eschatological teleology framed through that myth then will prove wholly appropriate to the method of the larger system of the Mishnah.

What, after all, makes a Messiah a false Messiah? In the Yerushalmi, it is not his claim to save Israel, but his claim to save Israel without the help of God. The meaning of the true Messiah is Israel's total submission, through the Messiah's gentle rule, to God's yoke and service. So God is not to be manipulated through Israel's humoring Heaven in rite and cult. The notion of keeping the commandments so as to please Heaven and get God to do what Israel wants—such a nakedly manipulative system is totally incongruent with the text at hand. Keeping the commandments as a mark of submission, loyalty, humility before God—it is this that marks the rabbinic system of salvation. So Israel does not "save itself."

The only choice is whether to cast one's fate into the hands of cruel, deceitful men, or to trust in the living God of mercy and love. We shall now see how this critical position is spelled out in the setting of discourse about the Messiah in the Yerushalmi of the Land of Israel.

Bar Kokhba, above all, exemplifies arrogance against God. He lost the war because of that arrogance. In particular, he ignored the authority of sages:

Y. Taanit 4:5

X.   J. Said R. Yohanan, "Upon orders of Caesar Hadrian, in Betar they killed eight hundred thousand."

    K. Said R. Yohanan, "There were eighty thousand pairs of trumpeteers surrounding Betar. Each one was in charge of a number of troops. Bar Kokhba was there, and he had two hundred thousand troops who, as a sign of loyalty, had cut off their little fingers.

    L. "Sages sent word to him, 'How long are you going to turn Israel into a maimed people?'

    M. "He said to them, 'How otherwise is it possible to test them?'

    N. "They replied to him, 'Whoever cannot uproot a cedar of Lebanon while riding on his horse will not be inscribed on your military rolls.'

    O. "So there were two hundred thousand who qualified in one way, and another two hundred thousand who qualified in another way."

    P. When he would go forth to battle, he would say, "Lord of the world! Do not help and do not hinder us! 'Hast thou not rejected us, O God? Thou dost not go forth, O God, with our armies'" (Psalm 60:10).

    Q. Three and a half years did Hadrian besiege Betar.

    R. R. Eleazar of Modiin would sit on sackcloth and ashes and pray every day, saying "Lord of the ages! Do not judge in accord with strict judgment this day!"

    S. Hadrian wanted to go to him. A Samaritan said to him, "Do not go to him, until I see what he is doing, and so hand over the city [of Betar] to you. ['Make peace . . . for you.']"

T. He got into the city through a drain pipe. He went and found R. Eleazar of Modiin standing and praying. He pretended to whisper something into his ear.

U. The townspeople saw [the Samaritan] do this and brought him to Bar Kokhba. They told him, "We saw this man having dealings with your friend."

V. [Bar Kokhba] said to him, "What did you say to him, and what did he say to you?"

W. He said to [the Samaritan], "If I tell you, then the king will kill me, and if I do not tell you, then you will kill me. It is better that the king kill me, and not you.

X. "[Eleazar] said to me, 'I should hand over my city.' ['I shall make peace . . .']."

Y. He turned to R. Eleazar of Modiin. He said to him, "What did this Samaritan say to you?"

Z. He replied, "Nothing."

AA. He said to him, "What did you say to him?"

BB. He said to him, "Nothing."

CC. [Bar Kokhba] gave [Eleazar] one good kick and killed him.

DD. Forthwith an echo came forth and proclaimed the following verse:

EE. "Woe to my worthless shepherd, who deserts the flock! May the sword smite his arm and his right eye! Let his arm be wholly withered, his right eye utterly blinded! (Zechariah 11:17).

FF. "You have murdered R. Eleazar of Modiin, the right arm of all Israel, and their right eye. Therefore may the right arm of that man wither, may his right eye be utterly blinded!"

GG. Forthwith Betar was taken, and Bar Kokhba was killed.

We notice two complementary themes. First, Bar Kokhba treats Heaven with arrogance, asking God to keep out of the way. Second, he treats an especially revered sage with a parallel arrogance. The sage had the power to preserve Israel. Bar Kokhba destroyed Israel's one protection. The result was inevitable.

Now in noticing the remarkable polemic in the story, in favor of sages' rule over that of Israelite strong men, we should not lose sight of the importance of the tale for our present argument about the Messiah and history.

First, the passage quite simply demonstrates an interest in narrating events other than those involving the Temple, on the one hand, or the sages in court, on the other. The story at hand and numerous others, not quoted here, testify to the emergence of a new category of history (or reemergence of an old one), namely, the history not of the supernatural cult, but of Israel the people. It indicates that, for the framers of those units of Yerushalmi that are not concerned with Mishnah-exegesis, and for the editors who selected materials for the final document, the history of Israel the people had now attained importance and demanded its rightful place. Once Israel's history thus reached centerstage, a rich heritage of historical thought would be invoked.

At that point, second, the Messiah, centerpiece of the history of salvation and hero of the tale, would emerge as a critical figure. The historical theory of the framers of the Yerushalmi passage at hand is stated very simply. In their view Israel had to choose between wars, either the war fought by Bar Kokhba or the "war for Torah." "Why had they been punished? It was because of the weight of the war, for they had not wanted to engage in the struggles over the meaning of the Torah" (Y. Taanit 3:9 XVI.I). Those struggles, ritual arguments about ritual matters, promised the one victory worth winning. Israel's history then would be written in terms of wars over the meaning of the Torah and the decision of the law.

True, the skins are new. But the wine is very old. For while we speak of sages and learning, the message is the familiar one. It is Israel's history that works out and expresses Israel's relationship with God. The critical dimension of Israel's life, therefore, is salvation, the definitive trait, movement in time from now to then. It follows that the paramount and organizing category is history and its lessons. As I suggested at the outset, in the Yerushalmi we witness, among the Mishnah's heirs, a striking reversion to biblical convictions about the centrality of history in the definition of Israel's reality. The heavy weight of prophecy, apocalyptic, and biblical historiography, with their emphasis upon salvation and on history as the indicator of Israel's salvation, stood against the Mishnah's quite separate thesis of what truly mattered. What, from their viewpoint, demanded description and analysis and required interpretation? It was the category of sanctification, for eternity. The true issue framed by history and apocalypse was how to move toward the foreordained end of salvation, how so to act in time as to reach salvation at the end of time. The Mishnah's teleology beyond time, its capacity to posit an eschatology lacking all place for a historical Messiah—these take

a position beyond the imagination of the entire antecedent sacred literature of Israel. Only one strand or stream, the priestly one, had ever taken
so extreme a position on the centrality of sanctification, the peripherality
of salvation. Wisdom had stood in between, with its own concerns,
drawing attention both to what happened and to what endured. But
what finally mattered to wisdom was not nature or supernature, but
rather abiding relationships in historical time.

This reversion by the authors of the Yerushalmi to Scripture's
paramount motifs, with Israel's history and destiny foremost among
them, forms a complement to the Yerushalmi's principal judgment upon
the Mishnah itself. For an important exegetical initiative of the Yerushalmi was to provide, for statements of the Mishnah, proof-texts deriving from Scripture. Whereas the framers of the Mishnah did not think
their statements required evidentiary support, the authors of the Yerushalmi's Mishnah-exegetical units of discourse took proof-texts drawn
from Scripture to be the prime necessity. Accordingly, at hand is yet
another testimony to the effort, among third- and fourth-century heirs of
the Mishnah, to draw that document back within the orbit of Scripture,
to "biblicize" what the Mishnah's authors had sent forth as a free-
standing and "nonbiblical" Torah.

The single most interesting indicator of the Yerushalmi's framers'
reversion to Scripture lies in the effort to go beyond systematizing biblical
events and showing their taxonomic status. Now they proposed to draw
lessons from biblical history. True, the framers of the Mishnah would not
have been surprised at their heirs' effort to find in ancient Israel's writings
lessons for the new day. They had done the same within the pages of the
Mishnah itself. A glance, for example, at the homiletical materials at M.
Taanit 2:1-4 shows how routinely they invoked biblical events, parallels,
analogies. But the Mishnah contains no counterpart to vast stretches of
the Yerushalmi's treatment of Scripture, specifically, its amplification of
biblical stories with a view to rewriting the repertoire of history of ancient
Israel. Evidence of that tendency will be found, for one example, in the
rabbinization of the Messiah. So now a single, if lengthy, example may
suffice to make the point. Before us is a striking instance of the amplification of the narrative of a major event in ancient Israelite history.

Y. Abodah Zarah 1:2

> I. V. Said R. Yudan, father of R. Mattenaiah, "The inten-
> tion of a verse of Scripture [such as is cited below]
> was only to make mention of the evil traits of Israel.

W. "'On the day of our king when Jeroboam was made king the princes became sick with the heat of wine; he stretched out his hand with mockers' (Hosea 7:5).

X. "On the day on which Jeroboam began to reign over Israel, all Israel came to him at dusk, saying to him, 'Rise up and make an idol.'

Y. "He said to them, 'It is already dusk. I am partly drunk and partly sober, and the whole people is drunk. But if you want, go and come back in the morning.'

Z. "This is the meaning of the following Scripture, 'For like an oven, their hearts burn with intrigue; all night their anger smolders; in the morning it blazes like a flaming fire' (Hosea 7:6)."

AA. "'All night their anger smolders.'

BB. "'In the morning it blazes like a flaming fire.'

CC. "In the morning they came to him. Thus did he say to them, 'I know what you want. But I am afraid of your Sanhedrin, lest it come and kill me.'

DD. "They said to him, 'We shall kill them.'

EE. "That is the meaning of the following verse: 'All of them are hot as an oven. And they devour their rulers' . . .'" (Hosea 7:7).

KK. When he would see an honorable man, he would set up against him two mockers, who would say to him, "Now what generation do you think is the most cherished of all generations?"

LL. He would answer them, "It was the generation of the wilderness which received the Torah."

MM. They would say to him, "Now did they themselves not worship an idol?"

NN. And he would answer them, "Now do you think that, because they were cherished, they were not punished for their deed?"

OO. And they would say to him, "Shut up! The king wants to do exactly the same thing. Not only so, but [the generation of the wilderness] only made one [calf], while [the king] wants to make two."

PP. [So the king took counsel and made two calves of gold] and he set up one in Bethel, and the other he put in Dan (1 Kings 12:29).

QQ. The arrogance of Jeroboam is what condemned him decisively.

RR. Said R. Yose bar Jacob, "It was at the conclusion of a sabbatical year that Jeroboam began to rule over Israel. That is the meaning of the following verse: '[And Moses commanded them]. At the end of every seven years, at the set time of the year of release, at the feast of booths, when all Israel comes to appear before the Lord your God at the place which He will choose, you shall read this law before all Israel in their hearing' (Deuteronomy 31:10-11).

SS. "[Jeroboam] said, 'I shall be called upon to read [the Torah, as Scripture requires]. If I get up and read first, they will say to me, 'The king of the place [in which the gathering takes place, namely, Jerusalem] comes first.' And if I read second, it is disrespectful to me. And if I do not read at all, it is a humiliation for me. And, finally, if I let the people go up, they will abandon me and go over to the side of Rehoboam the son of Solomon.'

TT. "That is the meaning of the following verse of Scripture: '[And Jeroboam said in his heart, Now the kingdom will turn back to the house of David;] if this people go up to offer sacrifices in the house of the Lord at Jerusalem, then the heart of this people will turn again to their Lord, to Rehoboam, king of Judah, and they will kill me and return to Rehoboam, king of Judah' (1 Kings 12:27-28).

UU. "What then did he do? 'He made two calves of gold' (1 Kings 12:28), and he inscribed on their heart, '. . . lest they kill you' [as counsel to his successors].

VV. "He said, 'Let every king who succeeds me look upon them.'"

Familiar motifs, such as the danger of arrogance, occur here, just as in passages in which sages explain events of their own day. The main point, however, is not to be missed. The extensive recounting of biblical tales, the interest in making points through the narrative of historical events—these do mark a break from the Mishnah's approach. For the framers of the Mishnah rarely found a use for the historical materials of Scripture. It is highly unusual to find in the Mishnah passages like this.

Interest in expanding biblical history, apart from the salvific focus imposed by that history, testifies to the process at hand: the renewal, in the pages of the Yerushalmi, of the age-old practice of homiletical retelling of biblical tales. The earlier document contains slight signs of such interest; its successor is rich in such evidence.

The reversion to the prophetic notion of learning the lessons of history carried in its wake reengagement with the Messiah-myth. The climax of the matter comes in an explicit statement that the practice of conduct required by the Torah will bring about the coming of the Messiah. That explanation of the purpose of the holy way of life, focused now upon the end of time and the advent of the Messiah, must strike us as surprising in light of the facts surveyed in an earlier chapter.

For the framers of the Mishnah had found it possible to construct a complete and encompassing teleology for their system with scarcely a single word about the Messiah's coming when the system would be perfectly achieved. So with their interest in explaining events and accounting for history, third- and fourth-century sages represented in the units of discourse at hand invoked what their predecessors had at best found of peripheral consequence to their system. The following contains the most striking expression of the viewpoint at hand.

Y. Taanit 1:1

X. J. "The oracle concerning Dumah. One is calling to me from Seir, 'Watchman, what of the night? Watchman, what of the night?' (Isaiah 21:11)."

K. The Israelites said to Isaiah, "O our Rabbi, Isaiah, What will come for us out of this night?"

L. He said to them, "Wait for me, until I can present the question."

M. Once he had asked the question, he came back to them.

N. They said to him, "Watchman, what of the night? What did the Guardian of the ages tell you?"

O. He said to them, "The watchman says 'Morning comes; and also the night. If you will inquire, inquire; come back again' (Isaiah 21:12)."

P. They said to him, "Also the night?"

Q. He said to them, "It is not what you are thinking. But there will be morning for the righteous, and night for the wicked, morning for Israel, and night for idolaters."

R. They said to him, "When?"

S. He said to them, "Whenever you want, He too wants [it to be]—if you want it, he wants it."

T. They said to him, "What is standing in the way?"

U. He said to them, "Repentance: 'Come back again' (Isaiah 21:12)."

V. R. Aha in the name of R. Tanhum b. R. Hiyya, "If Israel repents for one day, forthwith the son of David will come.

W. "What is the Scriptural basis? 'O that today you would hearken to his voice!' (Psalm 95:7)."

X. Said R. Levi, "If Israel would keep a single Sabbath in the proper way, forthwith the son of David will come.

Y. "What is the Scriptural basis for this view? 'Moses said, Eat it today, for today is a sabbath to the Lord; today you will not find it in the field' (Exodus 16:25).

Z. "And it says, 'For thus said the Lord God, the Holy One of Israel, "In returning and rest you shall be saved; in quietness and in trust shall be your strength." And you would not' (Isaiah 30:15)."

The discussion of the power of repentance would hardly have surprised a Mishnah-sage. What is new is at V–Z, the explicit linkage of keeping the law with achieving the end of time and the coming of the Messiah. That motif stands separate from the notions of righteousness and repentance, which surely do not require it. So the condition of "all Israel," a social category in historical time comes under consideration, and not only the status of individual Israelites in life and in death. The latter had formed the arena for Abot's account of the Mishnah's system's meaning. Now history as an operative category, drawing in its wake Israel as a social entity, comes once more on the scene. But, except for the Mishnah's sages, it had never left the stage.

We must not lose sight of the importance of this passage, with its emphasis on repentance, on the one side, and the power of Israel to reform itself, on the other. The Messiah will come any day that Israel makes it possible. If all Israel will keep a single Sabbath in the proper (rabbinic) way, the Messiah will come. If all Israel will repent for one day, the Messiah will come. "Whenever you want . . ." the Messiah will come. Now, two things are happening here. First, the system of religious observance, including study of Torah, is explicitly invoked as having salvific power. Second, the persistent hope of the people for the coming of the Messiah is linked to the system of rabbinic observance and belief. In this way, the austere program of the Mishnah, with no trace of a promise that the Messiah will come if and when the system is fully realized, finds a new development. A teleology lacking all eschatological dimensions here gives way to an explicitly messianic statement that the purpose of the law is to attain Israel's salvation: "If you want it, God wants it too." The one thing Israel commands is its own heart; the power it yet exercises is the power to repent. These suffice. The entire history of humanity will respond to Israel's will, to what happens in Israel's heart and soul. And, with the Temple in ruins, repentance can take place only within the heart and mind.

The framers of the Yerushalmi took over a document portraying a system centered upon sanctifying Israel through the creation of a world in stasis, wholly perfect within itself. They left behind them a document in which that original goal of sanctification in stasis competed with another. For within the pages of the Yerushalmi of the Land of Israel we find a second theory of what matters in Israel's life. A system centered on the salvation of Israel in a world moving toward a goal, a world to be perfected only at the conclusion of the journey through time, now came to full expression. So the bridge formed by the Yerushalmi of the Land of Israel leads from a world in which nothing happens but sanctification, to one in which everything happens en route to salvation at the end.

To understand the choices at hand, let us revert to the points of contrast and tension, the specification of opposites, in the materials now reviewed. These indicate the range of permissible choices, hence the boundaries of the reality posited by a given universe of discourse. If we were to administer a psychological test to the storytellers, asking them to state the opposite of a given word, the results cannot be in doubt. If we say, "This world," the storytellers who speak of kings and wars would answer, "the world to come," or "this age," and "the age to come." If, by contrast, we presented to storytellers who relate tales of sages, a given symbol of the natural world, they would reply with a counterpart—a symbol of the supernatural world. As we shall see in a moment, when (supernatural) rabbis die, for example, the (natural) world responds with miracles. In this sense, therefore, we confront two separate constructions of the world—polar possibilities. The one involves historical-messianic explanation of historical events, the other, supernatural explanation of natural ones. True, prayer may speak of either kind of occurrence. But at the climactic moment on the Day of Atonement, the prayer of the high priest turned to the natural world:

Y. Yoma 5:2

II. B. This was the prayer of the high priest on the Day of Atonement, when he left the Holy Place whole and in one piece: "May it be pleasing before You, Lord, our God of our fathers, that [a decree of] exile not be issued against us, not this day or this year, but if a decree of exile should be issued against us, then let it be exile to a place of Torah.

C. "May it be pleasing before You, Lord, our God and God of our fathers, that a decree of want not be issued against us, not this day of this year, but if a decree of want should be issued against us, then let it be a want of [the performance of] religious duties.

D. "May it be pleasing before You, Lord, our God and God of our fathers, that this year be a year of cheap food, full bellies, good business; a year in which the earth forms clods, then is parched so as to form scabs, and then moistened with dew,

E. "so that Your people, Israel, will not be in need of the help of one another.

F. "And do not heed the prayer of travelers [that it not rain]."

The high priest's prayer by itself obviously does not prove that, in all circumstances or contexts of sanctification, at issue are nature and supernature alone. But it does at least illustrate the self-evident association proposed at the outset. And the principal point must not be missed. One could speak of the ultimate resolution of Israel's present circumstance without invoking the name of the Messiah or the concept of events leading to a foreordained climax and conclusion with his coming at the end of time. Just as M. Sotah 9.15's author could refer to the resurrection of the dead and in the same breath speak of the coming of the Messiah, so too it remained possible to do this in the pages of the Yerushalmi.

The main point is that for the framers of the Mishnah, one could speculate about the meaning and end of the holy way of life of the holy people without any reference to the coming of the Messiah. For them and their heirs in the Yerushalmi of the Land of Israel the conception of redemption did not invariably invoke the salvific myth of the Messiah. Other units of discourse in the Yerushalmi carry forward this same treatment of the matter, as in the following.

Y. Yoma 3:2

> III. A. One time R. Hiyya the Elder and R. Simeon b. Ha-
> lapta were talking in the valley of Arabel at daybreak.
> They saw that the light of the morning star was
> breaking forth. Said R. Hiyya the Elder to R. Simeon
> b. Halapta, "Son of my master, this is what the re-
> demption of Israel is like—at first, little by little, but
> in the end it will go along and burst into light."
>
> B. "What is the Scriptural basis for this view? 'Rejoice
> not over me, O my enemy; when I fall, I shall rise;
> when I sit in darkness, the Lord will be a light to me'
> (Micah 7:8)."

How then does the Judaism of sanctification, as represented in the
Yerushalmi, take up events we should regard as historical? That is, how
is Israel to dispose of the events of the day, if not through fervent prayer
for the intervention of the Messiah? Bar Kokhba's way, sages maintained, was arrogant. What alternative did they offer? The answer is
that, within the framework of sanctification, as in the Mishnah, so in the
Yerushalmi, world-shaking events were treated as trivial, with history
converted into a symptom of the condition of private life, and great
events turned into epiphenomena within the framework of everyday
reality. Accordingly, within this system, as the Yerushalmi expresses it,
historical events play a decidedly subordinated role. Among the deeds
that do make history, mainly personal and private actions come to the
fore, not those that bear (to us) self-evident political and social consequence. Accordingly, historical events need not take a leading role in the
salvation of Israel—even when salvation is at issue. The "harsh decree"
may be averted through piety, charity, right attitude—surely not very
consequential deeds in the larger historical scheme of things.

Y. Taanit 2:1

> IX. A. Said R. Eleazar, "Three acts nullify the harsh decree,
> and these are they: prayer, charity, and repentance."
>
> B. And all three of them are to be derived from a single
> verse of Scripture:
>
> C. "If my people who are called by my name humble
> themselves, and pray and seek my face, and turn from
> their wicked ways, then I will hear from heaven, and

will forgive their sin and heal their land" (2 Chronicles 7:14).

D. "Pray"—this refers to prayer.

E. "And seek my face"—this refers to charity,

F. as you say, "As for me, I shall behold thy face in righteousness; when I awake, I shall be satisfied with beholding thy form" (Psalm 17:15).

G. "And turn from their wicked ways"—this refers to repentance.

H. Now if they do these things, what is written concerning them?

I. "Then I will hear from heaven and will forgive their sin and heal their land."

The forgiveness of sin draws in its wake prosperity, represented by the "healing of the land." These references therefore cannot apply solely to what happens to the individual. They deal with the fate of the whole of society. True, the harsh decree may come from the state; but the outcome is the same. Through repentance and its associated actions Israel can make its own history. In a statement like this, the issue of the coming of the Messiah simply plays no role. The historical-salvific-messianic does not merge with the timeless-sanctificatory-sagacious in materials of this kind; so far as I can see, within the pages of the Yerushalmi, no such union appears.

In Israel there were holy men who bore within themselves the power to save Israel. In this framework, the notion of the Messiah loses all pertinence. How so? Every sage, if sufficiently holy, could effect miracles for Israel. Whether salvation is at issue remains in doubt. For, in context, we deal with supernatural, not worldly, events: a miracle in nature, effected by a holy man, rather than a one-for-all historical resolution of Israel's situation, that is, "salvation" in the ordinary sense. The power of the holy or righteous man to save Israel is made explicit in the following:

Y. Yoma 1:1

V. D. Said R. Hiyya bar Ba, "The sons of Aaron died on the first day of Nisan. And why is their death called to mind in connection with the Day of Atonement?

E. "It is to indicate to you that just as the Day of Atonement effects expiation for Israel, so the death of the righteous effects atonement for Israel."

F. Said R. Ba bar Binah, "Why did the Scripture place
   the story of the death of Miriam side by side with the
   story of the burning of the red cow?

G. "It is to teach you that, just as the dirt of the red cow
   [mixed with water] effects atonement for Israel, so
   the death of the righteous effects atonement for
   Israel."

This brings us back to the doctrine of the Torah and salvation
through the Torah that we surveyed in the last chapter. For the sets of
opposites—time versus eternity, life versus death, nature versus supernature, on the one side, and history versus end of time, this world versus
time of the Messiah, death versus resurrection, on the other—need not
persist as separate and contradictory. The sage as holy man does his
work now and does it mainly through ongoing nature and unchanging
supernature. The Messiah—as distinct from a (any) sage—does his work
at the end of time. He does it once. In the resurrection of the dead, he
carries out a single, one-time action, by its nature one that need not be
repeated. He is a single and therefore unique figure, a kind of holy man to
be sure, but one of a kind, who performs a single, unique deed. Once a
messiah, in the sense of a high priest appointed for a given task to be
repeated many times, gives way to the Messiah, meaning, a man designed
to do a single task, never to be repeated, we leave the framework of the
Mishnah altogether.

This does not mean that people faced or even recognized a choice
between one teleology and another. It means that the eschatology beyond
history, the teleology beyond time, worked out in the Mishnah, stands
essentially asymmetrical to the parallel theories spelled out here. They
may be harmonized. They may sit side by side without colliding. But they
may not be represented as one and the same thing. They never meet.
And, in the canonical literature of Judaism, the two theories of where
things are heading scarcely intersect in a single pericope. The supernatural sage with his power over individual life and the natural world, and the
eschatological Messiah with his command over the people of Israel and
the whole of history—both within the model of the rabbi, in the image of
God—never meet, except when King David is perceived as Rabbi David.
And if truth be told, Rabbi David is mostly a rabbi, and only rarely a
messiah or the Messiah. If we did not know that David was the prototype
of the Messiah, the Yerushalmi would not have made us think so. In all,
the eschatological messiah is difficult to locate. "Messiah" defines a
category of holy man.

Epilogue

The Yerushalmi is a document of an age of transition, from ancient to medieval times. That judgment fully accords with established perspectives on both the age and the document itself. Historians of the West conventionally regard the two centuries with which we deal as the point at which ancient times end and the medieval age begins. *The Cambridge Ancient History*, vol. 12, for example, closes at 325 C.E., and the *Cambridge Medieval History*, vol. 1, begins at that same year. Along these lines, Salo Baron, the historian of the Jewish people, entitles his opening discussion on Talmudic history "Incipient Medievalism" and follows with his "World of the Talmud" and "Talmudic Law and Religion" (*A Social and Religious History of the Jews, vol. 2, Ancient Times*, pt. II). But that general observation does not guide us to the particular respect in which this age of transition is unusually interesting. What is distinctive to the history of Judaism, the Talmud itself, and what is general, the age of its creation and the ethos of the time, so correspond as to illuminate one another.

The Talmud of the Land of Israel turns out to lay its principal emphases upon precisely those things that the traits of the age and social imagination of the setting should have led us to expect. The Talmud's message speaks of how to attain certainty and authority in a time of profound change. The means lie in the person of the Talmudic sage. Salvation consists in becoming like him. In a unique idiom of its own, the Talmud says what people in general were saying in those days.

The principal development attested by the Yerushalmi is the figure of the rabbi, his centrality in the social and salvific world of the Jewish nation. The rabbi, after all, is the definitive phenomenon of the Judaism produced by him, called either by his title, Rabbinic Judaism, or by his

173

book, Talmudic Judaism, or by his theological authority, Classical Judaism, the authoritative or normative "classics" being the Talmuds and the
other writings of rabbis. Yet what appears particular and definitive turns
out upon second glance to be typical of its day and so quite unremarkable.
This is because in this introduction to the Yerushalmi we have pointed to
a phenomenon noticed in the same time but in quite other settings by
people who never saw the particular sources before us. Brown (1972) for
example, aptly describes, first, the transitional character of the age, and,
second, the critical role of a new type of man in that age. Because of the
centrality to my argument of what he says, I provide a sizable extract:

> The Late antique period has too often been dismissed as an age
> of disintegration, an age of otherworldliness in which sheltered
> souls withdrew from the crumbling society around them, to seek
> another, a Heavenly, city. No impression is further from the
> truth. Seldom has any period of European history littered the
> future with so many irremoveable institutions. The codes of
> Roman Law, the hierarchy of the Catholic Church, the idea of
> the Christian Empire, the monastery—up to the eighteenth
> century, men as far apart as Scotland and Ethiopia, Madrid and
> Moscow, still turned to these imposing legacies of the institu-
> tion-building of the Late Antique period for guidance as to how
> to organize their life in this world. I find it increasingly difficult
> to believe that these great experiments in social living were left
> there inadvertently by an age of dreamers, or that they happened
> through some last, tragic twitching of a supposed 'Roman ge-
> nius for organization'. They were, many of them, the new crea-
> tions of new men; and the central problem of Late Roman
> religious history is to explain why men came to act out their
> inner life through suddenly coagulating into new groups, and
> why they needed to find a new focus in the solidarities and sharp
> boundaries of the sect, the monastery, the orthodox Empire. The
> sudden flooding of the inner life into social forms: this is what
> distinguished the Late Antique period, of the third century
> onwards, from the Classical world. [p. 13]

It is not difficult to list the enduring and normative institutions of
Judaism created between the end of the second century and the end of
the fourth. But why bother to make a long list when the most important
were the two Talmuds! Still, even at this late stage of my argument, I
ought to spell out how the matrix to which the Talmuds testify, the

Judaism at hand, constituted the creation of a new kind of Israelite figure. So let us speak once more of this rabbi, this new man.

Standing at the end of Bar Kokhba's war and looking backward, we discern in the entire antecedent history of Israel no holy man analogous to the rabbi. There were diverse sorts of holy men. But the particular amalgam of definitive traits—charismatic clerk, savior-sage, lawyer-magician, and supernatural politician-bureaucrat—represented by the rabbi is not to be located in any former type of Israelite authority. Looking forward from the formation of the Talmud we rarely perceive a holy man wholly unlike the rabbi. None is out of touch with the rabbi's particular books. All present the knowledge of them as a source of legitimation at least until we reach (for a brief moment) the earliest phase of Hassidism in the eighteenth century. From the Talmud onward, Jewish authorities were authoritative because they knew the Talmud and conformed to its laws and modes of thought. The heretic opposed the Talmud and violated its laws. So whoever exercised power did so because, whatever other basis for authority he may have enjoyed, he was made holy by knowledge of the writings of rabbis of this period. So the Talmud was the creation, in Brown's words, of "new men." But what the new men made then endured as a foundation of the Jewish nation's social life from their time to our own. The rabbi as a distinctive Jewish authority persisted virtually alone for a millennium and a half and then, from the nineteenth century, in competition with other kinds of leaders, framed in competing modes of social and imaginative structure, lasted for another two hundred years thereafter, to the present day.

Accordingly, when I call "transitional" both the period at hand and the document under study, I mean, in particular, the period in which the Mishnah was made over into the Talmuds and in which the Mishnah's system was revised into the one the Talmuds put forth. These revolutionaries of late antiquity created something that stands, in its influence within its chosen society, equivalent to a Papacy, a Christian Empire, and a Caliphate—the other great institutions of late antiquity.

If I may now specify the single most interesting question presented to us by the formation of the rabbi as the definitive figure in Judaism, it is how to describe and interpret the relationship between the social events and conditions of the age as opposed to the development of the figure and authority of the rabbi. Brown defines the problem of study as an inquiry into "the nexus that links the inner experiences of men to the society around them" (p. 16). In the present context we should want to know two things. First, what made people want to become, or at least submit to the authority of, rabbis, as a particular kind of Jewish holy man–politician? Second, how did the rabbi interpret shared disciplines and sagacity, his program of accountable behavior and public responsibility, as the expression of his own inner life? We should like to relate content to context, public theology to inner anguish.

The sole source of facts in hand, unhappily, prevents us from answering either question. For the only evidence we have is the Talmud, not a private document but in essence and by definition the collective evidence of the generality of rabbis themselves. So we cannot deal with the former question. And, again by definition, rabbis never wrote their own individual books or spoke for themselves in particular. So we cannot take up the latter question either. The rabbi conforms to a single ideal type. In the sources, a rabbi scarcely reveals individual traits of mind or expression except within the collectively permitted framework of trivial points of difference. Not only does the rabbi emerge, therefore, as a completely public and available figure, lacking traits of individuation and substantial differentiation, he is also portrayed as an example of social, and hence common, virtue.

This judgment requires some qualification. For while the rabbi of the Talmud is never an individual, he also is never merely a conventional or convenient name on which to hang a random opinion. True, he is one of a type, not wholly individuated. But he also is not merely a genus, but, in himself, a specimen of a genus—a genius. A contrast is to be drawn between the Mishnah and the Talmud. One may differentiate Mishnaic rabbis only by idiosyncratic opinions on unimportant things. By contrast, we can easily distinguish one Talmudic authority from another on a much broader range of points of difference and individuation. Each one typifies. But the range of choice is broader and more interesting. So the Talmud differs from the Mishnah in this important aspect too. Its authors, and not only the things they say, play a major role in the document. Thus while sages in the Mishnah have names but no faces, opinions but no biographies, rabbis in the Talmud not only say things but also do things. They are given flesh-and-blood lives and, in the anachronistic nature of things, so are their Mishnaic predecessors. The power to change the world, not merely judge or describe it, was the rabbi's. The power of the rabbi extended back to Moses' Scripture, forward to the Messiah. He was the link, his word the guarantee. The lifeless names of the Mishnah can scarcely compete.

The Mishnah came forth confidently on its own, only to be chained to a mass of Scriptural proof-texts. So the new Mishnah was made old, a new version of ancient Scripture, and the fresh transformed into avatar and continuator of the solely authoritative. Perhaps that is how matters had to be in the logic of things. But it is also how things were in the age itself. For, as Brown describes matters, the shift from the second century to the fourth was a time in which people confronted "a mounting tension between their inner and their outer life, between the demands of their personal experience and the patterns of life so confidently handed down to them by an ancient society" (p. 11).

The Mishnah was made over into a mere amplification and specification of general rules of Scripture, supplied with proof-texts for most of its propositions. The Mishnah, for its part, defined the program of the Talmud. The exegesis of its specific laws form the focus of interest and discourse; in the Talmud little else takes place. The authority of Scripture through the specification of the Mishnah then was made to reach into the obscure and unimportant details of the life of Israel everywhere, under all imaginable conditions and circumstances. If the Mishnah speaks mainly of the Temple, on the one side, and public life, on the other, the Talmud addresses an inner world of privacy, both in petty transactions and in people's dreams and fears, to which the Mishnah is oblivious. So the movement from the Mishnah to the Talmud belies the formal design of the Talmud as a mere commentary to, and extension of, the Mishnah. In fact, what takes shape is a new construction, in literary and conceptual terms alike, built with the bricks and mortar of the old. The Talmud is indeed an amplification and extension of the Mishnah. But the net result of the Talmud is a kind of Judaism asymmetrical with the Mishnah, off-center.

The Mishnah governs what the rabbi knows. But it is the rabbi who speaks about the Mishnah. He imposes his voice by breaking the Mishnah down into bits and pieces, then doing what he wants with some of them. Like a good apprentice to an artist, the rabbi copied carefully. He faithfully memorized the Mishnah and subserviently mastered its principles and details. Then he went and made his own freehand picture. In his masterpiece one discerns the technique of color and brushstrokes of his master. But seeing it whole, we gaze upon what is original to the apprentice, now shown to be an artist in his own right.

The most important fact in the Talmud is its anonymous, monotonous, uniform voice, its "rabbi." The critical actor is the rabbi as authority on earth and intermediary of supernatural power. If we did not know that the Talmud came from the time and place from which it comes, knowledge of those two definitive facts of this document, joined with familiarity with the world of late antiquity, should have made us guess so. For, as I said at the outset, the rabbi, so particular to Judaism and distinctive to the Talmud, also is typical of his age. He presents a version, for Judaism, of what was wholly commonplace in the world at large. This is how Brown (1971) describes matters:

> The idea of the holy man holding the demons at bay and bending the will of God by his prayers came to dominate Late Antique society. In many ways, the idea is as new as the society itself. For it placed a man, a "man of power," in the centre of people's imagination. Previously, the classical world had tended to think of its religion in terms of things. Ancient religion had revolved round great temples, against whose ancient stones even the most impressive priest had paled into insignificance; the gods had spoken impersonally at their oracle-sites; their ceremonies assumed a life in which the community, the city, dwarfed the individual. In the fourth and fifth centuries, however, the individual, as a "man of power," came to dwarf the traditional communities. . . . In the popular imagination, the emergence of the holy man at the expense of the temple marks the end of the classical world. [pp. 11–16]

Brown (1978) elaborates on this matter in the following way.

> What changed in no uncertain manner . . . between the second and the fifth centuries, were men's views as to where exactly this "divine power" was to be found on earth and, consequently, on what terms access to it could be achieved. . . .
>
>   In the period between 200 and 400, Mediterranean men came to accept, in increasing numbers and with increasing enthusiasm, the idea that this "divine power" did not only manifest itself directly to the average individual or through perennially established institutions: rather "divine power" was represented on earth by a limited number of exceptional human agents, who had been empowered to bring it to bear among their fellows by reason of a relationship with the supernatural that was personal to them, stable and clearly perceptible to fellow believers. . . .
>
>   What gives Late Antiquity its special flavor is precisely the claims of human beings . . . to vest a fellow human being with powers and claims to loyalty associated with the supernatural, and especially a human being whose claim was not rendered unchallengeable by obvious coercive powers, is a momentous decision for a society made up of small face-to-face groups to make. [pp. 11–16]

There is scarcely need to point out how the Talmud's figure of the rabbi conforms to Brown's account of the prevailing imagination of the age. The rabbi, mediating divine power, yet highly individual, became the center and the focus of the supernatural life of Israel. In the age at hand, that was his view, perhaps not widely held, and not shared at all by other Big Men. But in the time to come, the rabbi would become Israel's model of sanctification, the Jew's promise of ultimate salvation. This is why from then to nearly now, whatever Judaism there would ever be properly came to be called rabbinic.

The Talmud effects an astonishing parallelism between Scripture and sage. In a word, the talmud brings forth the rabbi as Scripture incarnate, therefore (completing the trilogy) the hope and salvation of Israel. Out of the union of the Torah and the person of the rabbi, the messianic and salvific faith, Rabbinic Judaism, was born. What worldly use has this faith, created in the matrix of the late antiquity, served, and how has the Jewish sector of the civilization of the West drawn nourishment and hope from it? What the rabbi of our Talmud bequeathed to Israel and the West in the end is a vision of man in the image of God, a model for what a man can be: not mud alone but mind as well. His legacy served to exalt man's unique powers of thought, to order his daily routine and endow it with a wonderful sense of its formal perfection. So the national historical life of Israel was matched by and joined to the local and private life of the village. The whole served as a paradigm of ultimate perfection, sanctification—hence salvation. (True, from his time to ours, the Talmud's rabbi as model served for only half of Israel, the male half. Yet that is our problem, not the Talmud's, which, in this regard, alas, proved no better than its day, if not much worse.) The power of the Talmud's vision endures for an age with the lesser view of humanity. Ours is diminished faith in the human capacity of rationality to attain orderly rules for sanctification in the everyday and so to gain salvation in the end of days.

REFERENCES

Brown, Peter. (1971). *World of Late Antiquity*. New York: Norton.

———. (1972). *Religion and Society in the Age of St. Augustine*. New York: Harper & Row.

———. (1978). *The Making of Late Antiquity*. Cambridge, MA: Harvard University Press.

Acknowledgments
and Bibliography

The translations derive from my book *The Talmud of the Land of Israel*, cited below. In Chapters One, Two, Three, and the Epilogue, I have revised studies that originally appeared in *The Talmud of the Land of Israel. 35. Introduction, Taxonomy*; and *Judaism and Society: The Evidence of the Yerushalmi*, and Chapter Four draws heavily upon my *Foundations of Judaism: Method, Teleology, Doctrine. II. Messiah in Context. Israel's History and Destiny in Formative Judaism*, and also upon *The Christian and Judaic Invention of History*. My thanks go to the copyright holders for permission to reproduce, with substantial revisions, abstracts from those books, publication data for which are given below. A full bibliography for the Yerushalmi by Baruch M. Bokser is in the work edited by me, *The Study of Ancient Judaism*. New York: Ktav, 1981. I. *The Study of Ancient Judaism: Mishnah, Midrash, Siddur*. II. *The Study of Ancient Judaism: The Palestinian and Babylonian Talmuds*. [Second printing: 1988]. My translation is as follows:

The Talmud of the Land of Israel. A Preliminary Translation and Explanation. Chicago: The University of Chicago Press, 1982-1989. IX-XII, XIV-XV, XVII-XXXV.

    XXXIV.   *Horayot. Niddah.* 1982.
    XXXIII.   *Abodah Zarah.* 1982.
    XXXII.   *Shebuot.* 1983.
    XXXI.   *Sanhedrin. Makkot.* 1984.

XXX.   *Baba Batra*. 1984.
XXIX.   *Baba Mesia*. 1984.
XXVIII.   *Baba Qamma*. 1984.
XXVII.   *Sotah*. 1984.
XXVI.   *Qiddushin*. 1984.
XXV.   *Gittin*. 1985.
XXIV.   *Nazir*. 1985.
XXIII.   *Nedarim*. 1985.
XXII.   *Ketubot*. 1985.
XXI.   *Yebamot*. 1986.
XX.   *Hagigah. Moed Qatan*. 1986.
XIX.   *Megillah*. 1987.
XVIII.   *Besah. Taanit*. 1987.
XVII.   *Sukkah*. 1988.
XV.   *Sheqalim*. 1990.
XIV.   *Yoma*. 1990.
XII.   *Erubin*. 1990.
XI.   *Shabbat*. 1991.
X.   *Orlah. Bikkurim*. 1991.
IX.   *Hallah*. 1991.

Edited: *In the Margins of the Yerushalmi. Notes on the English Translation*. Chico: Scholars Press for Brown Judaic Studies, 1983.

A bibliography of works of mine in which the Yerushalmi appears prominently follows.

Death and Birth of Judaism. The Impact of Christianity, Secularism, and the Holocaust on Jewish Faith. New York: Basic Books, 1987.

Formative Judaism. Religious, Historical, and Literary Studies. First Series. Chico: Scholars Press for Brown Judaic Studies, 1982.

Formative Judaism. Religious, Historical, and Literary Studies. Second Series. Chico: Scholars Press for Brown Judaic Studies, 1983.

Formative Judaism. Religious, Historical, and Literary Studies. Third Series. Torah, Pharisees, and Rabbis. Chico: Scholars Press for Brown Judaic Studies, 1983.

Formative Judaism. Religious, Historical, and Literary Studies. Fourth Series. Problems of Classification and Composition. Chico: Scholars Press for Brown Judaic Studies, 1984.

Formative Judaism. Religious, Historical, and Literary Studies. Fifth Series. Revisioning the Written Records of a Nascent Religion. Chico: Scholars Press for Brown Judaic Studies, 1985.

Formative Judaism. Religious, Historical, and Literary Studies. Sixth Series. Atlanta: Scholars Press for Brown Judaic Studies, 1989.

In Search of Talmudic Biography. The Problem of the Attributed Saying. Chico: Scholars Press for Brown Judaic Studies, 1984. Reprise and reworking of materials in *Eliezer ben Hyrcanus. The Tradition and the Man.*

Invitation to the Talmud. A Teaching Book. New York: Harper & Row, 1973. Second printing, 1974. Paperback edition, 1975. Reprinted: 1982. Second edition, completely revised, San Francisco: Harper & Row, 1984. Paperback edition: 1988.

Judaism in the Matrix of Christianity. Philadelphia: Fortress Press, 1986. British edition, Edinburgh: T. & T. Collins, 1988. Dutch translation: Hilversum: Gooi & Sticht, 1989. Italian translation: Torino: Editrice Marietti, 1990.

Judaism and its Social Metaphors. Israel in the History of Jewish Thought. New York: Cambridge University Press, 1988.

Judaism in Society: The Evidence of the Yerushalmi. Toward the Natural History of a Religion. Chicago: The University of Chicago Press, 1983. *Choice*, "Outstanding Academic Book List, 1984-1985."

Judaism and Christianity in the Age of Constantine. Issues of the Initial Confrontation. Chicago: The University of Chicago Press, 1987.

Judaism: The Classical Statement. The Evidence of the Bavli. Chicago: The University of Chicago Press, 1986. *Choice*, "Outstanding Academic Book List, 1987."

Editor: *Judaisms and their Messiahs in the Beginning of Christianity.* New York: Cambridge University Press, 1987. [Edited with William Scott Green and Ernest S. Frerichs.]

Major Trends in Formative Judaism. First Series. Society and Symbol in Political Crisis. Chico: Scholars Press for Brown Judaic Studies, 1983.

Major Trends in Formative Judaism. Second Series. Texts, Contents, and Contexts. Chico: Scholars Press for Brown Judaic Studies, 1984.

Major Trends in Formative Judaism. Third Series. The Three Stages in the Formation of Judaism. Chico: Scholars Press for Brown Judaic Studies, 1985. Italian translation: Casale Monferrato: Editrice Marietti, 1989.

Editor: *Scriptures of the Oral Torah. Sanctification and Salvation in the Sacred Books of Judaism.* San Francisco: Harper & Row, 1987. Jewish Book Club Selection, 1988.

Self-Fulfilling Prophecy: Exile and Return in the History of Judaism. Boston: Beacon Press, 1987.

The Talmud of the Land of Israel: A Preliminary Translation and Explanation. Chicago: The University of Chicago Press, 1983: XXXV. *Introduction. Taxonomy.*

The Religious Study of Judaism. Description, Analysis, Interpretation. Vol. One. Lanham: University Press of America, 1986. *Studies in Judaism* series.

The Religious Study of Judaism. Description, Analysis, Interpretation. Vol. Two. *The Centrality of Context.* Lanham: University Press of America, 1986. *Studies in Judaism* series.

The Religious Study of Judaism. Description, Analysis, Interpretation. Vol. Three. *Context, Text, and Circumstance.* Lanham: University Press of America, 1987. *Studies in Judaism* series.

The Religious Study of Judaism. Description, Analysis, Interpretation. Vol. Four. *Ideas of History, Ethics, Ontology, and Religion in Formative Judaism.* Lanham: University Press of America, 1988. *Studies in Judaism* series.

The Foundations of Judaism. Philadelphia: Fortress, 1988. Abridged edition of the foregoing trilogy.

The Foundations of Judaism. Method, Teleology, Doctrine. Philadelphia: Fortress Press, 1983–1985: I–III. I. *Midrash in Context. Exegesis in Formative Judaism.* Second printing: Atlanta: Scholars Press for Brown Judaic Studies, 1988.

The Foundations of Judaism. Method, Teleology, Doctrine. Philadelphia: Fortress Press, 1983–1985: I–III. II. *Messiah in Context. Israel's History and Destiny in Formative Judaism.* Second printing: Lanham: University Press of America, 1988. *Studies in Judaism* series.

The Foundations of Judaism. Method, Teleology, Doctrine. Philadelphia: Fortress Press, 1983–1985: I–III. III. *Torah: From Scroll to Symbol in Formative Judaism.* Second printing: Atlanta: Scholars Press for Brown Judaic Studies, 1988.

The Bavli and Its Sources: The Question of Tradition in the Case of Tractate Sukkah. Atlanta: Scholars Press for Brown Judaic Studies, 1987.

The Oral Torah. The Sacred Books of Judaism. An Introduction. San Francisco: Harper & Row, 1985. Paperback: 1987. B'nai B'rith Jewish Book Club Selection, 1986.

The Incarnation of God: The Character of Divinity in Formative Judaism. Philadelphia: Fortress Press, 1988.

The Christian and Judaic Invention of History. [Edited with William Scott Green]. Atlanta: Scholars Press for American Academy of Religion, 1989. *Studies in Religion* series.

The Peripatetic Saying: The Problem of the Thrice-Told Tale in Talmudic Literature. Chico: Scholars Press for Brown Judaic Studies, 1985. Reprise and reworking of materials in *Development of a Legend. Rabbinic Traditions about the Pharisees before 70.* I-III.

The Formation of the Jewish Intellect. Making Connections and Drawing Conclusions in the Traditional System of Judaism. Atlanta: Scholars Press for Brown Judaic Studies, 1988.

The Making of the Mind of Judaism. Atlanta: Scholars Press for Brown Judaic Studies, 1987.

Vanquished Nation, Broken Spirit. The Virtues of the Heart in Formative Judaism. New York: Cambridge University Press, 1987. Jewish Book Club Selection, 1987.

Why No Gospels in Talmudic Judaism? Atlanta: Scholars Press for Brown Judaic Studies, 1988.

Writing with Scripture: The Authority and Uses of the Hebrew Bible in the Torah of Formative Judaism. Philadelphia: Fortress Press, 1989.

Index

About the Author

Dr. Jacob Neusner is Distinguished Research Professor of Religious Studies at University of South Florida, Tampa. The recipient of numerous scholarships, fellowships, awards, and research grants, Dr. Neusner is the author or editor of over 500 books on Jewish themes, including *The Foundations of the Theology of Judaism, The Mishnah: An Introduction, The Midrash: An Introduction,* and *A Rabbi Talks with Jesus: An Intermillennial Interfaith Exchange.*